A YEAR WITH JESUS

A YEAR WITH JESUS

Daily Readings and Meditations

EUGENE H. PETERSON

Discipleship Inside Out®

NavPress is the publishing ministry of The Navigators, an international Christian organization and leader in personal spiritual development. NavPress is committed to helping people grow spiritually and enjoy lives of meaning and hope through personal and group resources that are biblically rooted, culturally relevant, and highly practical.

**For a free catalog go to www.NavPress.com
or call 1.800.366.7788 in the United States or 1.800.839.4769 in Canada.**

For Lynn

In gratitude for gifts named and unnamed

A Year with Jesus

The goal of spending a year with Jesus is to learn how to pray. Our prayers do not start with us. They start with Jesus. Before we ever open our mouths in prayer, Jesus is praying for us. Despite much talk to the contrary, there are no secrets to living the Christian life. No prerequisite attitudes. No conditions more or less favorable to pursing the Way. Anyone can do this, from any place, starting at any time. But it is only possible through prayer. We can only pray our lives into the way of following Jesus.

Prayer provides the primary language for everything that takes place in the way of Jesus. If we go to a shopping mall in North America, we speak English to get what we want. If we go to a restaurant in France, we speak French to order our meal. If we travel to Greece, we speak Greek to find our way to the Acropolis. And when we become personally involved with Jesus, we pray. We pray because it is the only language we have for speaking to the God revealed in Jesus. It is also the only language we have for listening to the commands and blessings and guidance that God provides in Jesus. God is nothing if not personal. Both God and we humans are most personal, most characteristically our unique selves, in our use of language. The language between God and us is called prayer.

What I want to insist on is that prayer is not something added on to the Christian life (or any life, for that matter). We cannot specialize in prayer any more than we can specialize in life. We cannot abstract prayer from our living, or isolate instances of prayer and study them under laboratory conditions. It is the language in which our lives are lived out, nurtured, developed, revealed, and informed. The language in which we believe, love, explore, seek, and find. There are no shortcuts or detours: Prayer is the cradle language among all those who are "born anew" and grow up to follow Jesus.

Prayer is a way of living. It is not a subject to be studied. It is not a technique to be learned. It is a life lived in response to God. We do not learn *about* prayer, we learn *to* pray; and the prayer, as it turns out, is never *just* prayer, but involves every dimension of our lives—eating, drinking, loving, working, walking, reading, and singing. The way we follow Jesus must be internalized and embodied. That is what prayer does, gets Jesus inside us, gets his Spirit into our muscles and reflexes. There is no other way. Judas followed Jesus with his feet all over Palestine, but it never got inside him. Peter listened with his ears to everything Jesus said and spoke with his mouth the deepest truth about Jesus ("You're the Christ"), but when he cut off the ear of Malchus in Gethsemane, we know that he hadn't learned that way of life from Jesus (see Matthew 16:16; John 18:10).

But because in our secularized society prayer is often associated with what people of "spiritual" interests pursue or with formal acts conducted by professional leaders, it is necessary from time to time to call attention to the fact that prayer is the street language that we use with Jesus as he walks the streets with us. We can't put off prayer until we "get good at it." It is the only language available to us as we bring our unique and particular selves, "just as we are without one plea," into daily, hourly conversation with God, who comes "just as he is" in Jesus.[1]

Following Jesus necessarily means getting his words and ways into our everyday lives. It is not enough simply to recognize and approve his ways and get started in the right direction. Everything about Jesus is there to be embraced by our imaginations and assimilated into our habits—*believed* and *lived*. This takes place only as we *pray* while reading the story of Jesus, pray what we see Jesus doing, pray what we hear Jesus saying, pray the questions we have, pray the commands and promises and invitations that come to us in this story, pray the difficulties we encounter on the way.

Jesus' praying was never something apart from his living. We cannot isolate his praying from his living. His whole life is the context for understanding and then participating in his praying. It is the same with us: Our entire lives provide circumstances and stuff for our prayers.

Jesus' life cannot be imposed from without. It cannot be copied. It must be shaped from within. This shaping takes place in prayer. The practice of prayer is the primary way by which the life of Jesus comes to permeate our entire lives so that we walk spontaneously and speak rhythmically in the fluidity and fluency of holiness. Left to ourselves we are fragmented and distracted people, jerky and spasmodic. Sin does that to us. The more object-like, the more thing-like, the more impersonal we become, the more disengaged we are from our God-created humanity and from the God-created world around us. Prayer, as the Spirit prays within us (and he most certainly does, whether we are aware of it or not—see Romans 8:19-26), recovers our original place in creation so that we can live robustly in the world. Prayer in conversation with Jesus involves us firsthand in the grand reconciliation going on in Christ, setting us free for relational intimacies with family and friends, the heavens above us, and the earth under our feet (see Colossians 1:15-23). When we embrace the companionship of the praying Jesus, "Everything becomes a You and nothing remains an It."[2]

We pray with Jesus; Jesus prays with us. Day-by-day, week-by-week, month-by-month, Jesus—God with us—is prayed into the details of our lives, and God's salvation is formed in us.

In order to provide this text for your prayers and Jesus' prayers—a true conversation—I have taken the stories and words of Jesus from the gospels of Saint Matthew and Saint John and spread them across a 365-day sequence of reading, reflection, and prayer. I interrupt Matthew two chapters from the end in order to let John provide the ending, and a most magnificent ending it is. My intent is that your reading of Jesus turns into praying with Jesus, keeping his delightful company as lover and friend.

Family Tree

The family tree of Jesus Christ, David's son, Abraham's son.

MATTHEW 1:1

Three names mark key points in God's salvation work: Abraham, father of the faithful; David, the man after God's own heart; Jesus, the son of God, who summed up Abraham and David and revealed all that God is for us.

Why are ancestors important?

You come, Jesus, out of a history thick with names. Names — not dates, not events — signal the junctures in which you single out me and others for personal love and responsibility. Named, I now name your name in trust and gratefulness: Jesus. Amen.

. . . Who Gave Birth to Jesus

Abraham had Isaac, Isaac had Jacob, Jacob had Judah and his brothers, Judah had Perez and Zerah (the mother was Tamar), Perez had Hezron, Hezron had Aram, Aram had Amminadab, Amminadab had Nahshon . . . Eliud had Eleazar, Eleazar had Matthan, Matthan had Jacob, Jacob had Joseph, Mary's husband, the Mary who gave birth to Jesus, the Jesus who was called Christ. There were fourteen generations from Abraham to David, another fourteen from David to the Babylonian exile, and yet another fourteen from the Babylonian exile to Christ.

MATTHEW 1:2-4,15-17

The biblical fondness for genealogical lists is not dull obscurantism, it is an insistence on the primacy and continuity of people. Each name is a burnished link connecting God's promises to his fulfillments in the chain of people who are the story of God's mercy.

Which of these names stands out for you?

Some of these names I don't recognize at all, God. And that is reassuring! I don't have to be an Abraham or a David to be included in this salvation litany. My ordinariness is as essential as another's extraordinariness. Thank you. Amen.

By Tamar

Judah had Perez and Zerah (the mother was Tamar), Perez had Hezron, Hezron had Aram . . . Salmon had Boaz (his mother was Rahab), Boaz had Obed (Ruth was the mother), Obed had Jesse, Jesse had David, and David became king. David had Solomon (Uriah's wife was the mother).

MATTHEW 1:3,5-6

Four names in the list are a surprise: Tamar, Rahab, Ruth, and the wife of Uriah (Bathsheba). Each of these names represents a person who was exploited, or downtrodden, or an outsider — the misused, the immoral, the foreign. Jesus' genealogy doesn't prove racial or moral purity, but redemptive range. God's salvation work is inclusive, not exclusive.

What do you know of each of these women?

Do I have enough confidence, Lord, in your inventive and incorporative will, to believe that you will use unattractive, immoral, and unlovely people as well as the glamorous and virtuous and admirable? That is hard to believe, but the evidence is impressive. Help my unbelief. Amen.

Forty-Two Generations

Jacob had Joseph, Mary's husband, the Mary who gave birth to Jesus, the Jesus who was called Christ. There were fourteen generations from Abraham to David, another fourteen from David to the Babylonian exile, and yet another fourteen from the Babylonian exile to Christ.

MATTHEW 1:16-17

The list concludes with a name (Jesus) plus a title (Christ). The forty-two generations conclude with Jesus, who is given the title Christ (in Hebrew, Messiah), the person whom God anoints to accomplish our salvation. The final name is simultaneously a human life and a divine work.

What does the name Jesus Christ mean to you?

I see, Father, that you do not simply permit names to accumulate at random, but that you shape lives. There is a design, and there is a goal. Enter my earth-conditioned existence and shape eternity in me. Amen.

The Birth of Jesus

The birth of Jesus took place like this. His mother, Mary, was engaged to be married to Joseph. Before they came to the marriage bed, Joseph discovered she was pregnant. (It was by the Holy Spirit, but he didn't know that.)

MATTHEW 1:18

There is a combination of old and new in this birth story: traditional angels, visions, prophecies; there is also the miraculously innovative divine Spirit. There are historical data; there is also virginal conception.

Why is the virgin birth significant?

I am not satisfied with reading about your birth, Lord, I want to be in on it. Take the ancient history of my childhood and religion and put it to use. Make the birth of Christ as vivid and actual in me as it was in Mary. Amen.

Joseph, a Noble Man

Joseph, chagrined but noble, determined to take care of things quietly so Mary would not be disgraced. While he was trying to figure a way out, he had a dream. God's angel spoke in the dream: "Joseph, son of David, don't hesitate to get married. Mary's pregnancy is Spirit-conceived. God's Holy Spirit has made her pregnant."

MATTHEW 1:19-20

Joseph thought that "noble" involved doing the proper thing; he was about to find out that it was also being the right person. The word "noble" changes meaning in this event, a change from loyalty to a moral tradition to obedience to a divine person. Faith crowds out duty and wisdom as the dynamic of the "noble man."

How would you describe a noble person?

Father, there is no way I can respond appropriately to your presence unless you break into my imagination in a dream. I will pray expectantly, open to your vision. How else will I receive guidance for becoming a noble person? Amen.

Name Him Jesus

"She will bring a son to birth, and when she does, you, Joseph, will name him Jesus—'God saves'—because he will save his people from their sins." This would bring the prophet's embryonic sermon to full term.

MATTHEW 1:21-22

Mary's work was giving birth; Joseph's work was naming. Much attention has been given, appropriately enough, to Mary. But why the avoidance of Joseph? He was set apart for the priestly-poetic task of naming a character and defining a destiny.

What does the name Jesus mean?

Jesus, your name defines the gospel: not a model that I can admire and follow, but a Savior entering the world of my troubled heart and doing something—saving me. Amen.

The Prophet's Embryonic Sermon

This would bring the prophet's embryonic sermon to full term: "Watch for this—a virgin will get pregnant and bear a son; They will name him Immanuel (Hebrew for 'God is with us')."

MATTHEW 1:22-23

A deep, contrapuntal resonance reverberates between Isaiah's prophecy and Mary's pregnancy. Half-formed expectations take shape embryonically. Obscurely imagined messianic hopes get a character and a name.

Read and compare Isaiah 7:1-14.

There are promises and longings out of my past, my infancy and childhood, O God, that you fulfill in the birth of Jesus in my life. Complete the fulfillment, being with me in your fullness. Amen.

He Did . . .

Then Joseph woke up. He did exactly what God's angel commanded in the dream: He married Mary. But he did not consummate the marriage until she had the baby. He named the baby Jesus.

MATTHEW 1:24-25

It is one thing to have dreams, another thing to act on them. Joseph both dreamed and acted—a perfect model of obedience. He affirmed the action of the Holy Spirit in his closest personal relationship, he refrained from interfering in the divine process, and he did what he was told.

Why is Joseph important in your life?

When I observe the action of this mature, free man, Lord—the reckless involvement, the disciplined restraint, the plain obedience, and all of it woven together in one coherent righteous action—I know that I, too, can live in daring obedience before you. Amen.

Jesus/Herod

After Jesus was born in Bethlehem village, Judah territory—this was during Herod's kingship—a band of scholars arrived in Jerusalem from the East.

MATTHEW 2:1

The two names, Jesus and Herod, are in contrast. The general ("during Herod's kingship") gives way to the particular ("Jesus was born"). Kingship comes into focus. Rule is personalized. Geography and politics slip into mere background as Jesus centers all history.

What are you most interested in?

God, when I see how kings and nations slip into the shadows at Jesus' birth, I see that I will do well not to become engrossed in either of them. It will not be by excavating Bethlehem or by analyzing Herod, but by worshiping you that my life will find center and purpose. Amen.

A Band of Scholars

After Jesus was born in Bethlehem village, Judah territory — this was during Herod's kingship — a band of scholars arrived in Jerusalem from the East. They asked around, "Where can we find and pay homage to the newborn King of the Jews? We observed a star in the eastern sky that signaled his birth. We're on pilgrimage to worship him."

MATTHEW 2:1-2

A band of scholars were experts in the movement of the stars and signs in the heavens. Their inquiry thrust the provincial village into a cosmic concern. It was not scientific data they were searching out, but a person to worship. True wisdom is not gathering information; it is adoration of God's revealed truth.

What is your favorite story of these scholars?

Teach me this wisdom, Lord: I often treat worship as a means to some other end, intellectual or material. But these men didn't come to the Christ as scholars to learn more, or as wealthy tycoons to amass more plunder; they came to worship. Amen.

He Was Terrified

When word of their inquiry got to Herod, he was terrified — and not Herod alone, but most of Jerusalem as well. Herod lost no time. He gathered all the high priests and religion scholars in the city together and asked, "Where is the Messiah supposed to be born?" They told him, "Bethlehem, Judah territory. The prophet Micah wrote it plainly."

MATTHEW 2:3-5

While the magi approached the birth of Jesus with reverential awe, Herod, hearing the news, was full of dread. It is possible to fashion values and goals so defiant of God that any rumor of his reality shakes our foundation.

What are your values?

Prevent, O God, the Herodian spirit from filtering into my life; the spirit that uses religion to protect itself, and is jealous of any hint of rivalry, responds to your Spirit only with suspicious fear. Amen.

No Longer Bringing Up the Rear

They told him, "Bethlehem, Judah territory. The prophet Micah wrote it plainly: 'It's you, Bethlehem, in Judah's land, no longer bringing up the rear. From you will come the leader who will shepherd-rule my people, my Israel.'"

MATTHEW 2:5-6

Even obscure items of geography—little Bethlehem, for instance—by prophetic designation play their part in the messianic history. The village is now one of the best known on earth. Significance comes not from size but from the Savior.

Where is Bethlehem?

"O holy Child of Bethlehem, descend to us, we pray; cast out our sin, and enter in, be born in us today. We hear the Christmas angels the great glad tidings tell; O come to us, abide with us, our Lord Emmanuel."[3] Amen.

Leave No Stone Unturned

Herod then arranged a secret meeting with the scholars from the East. Pretending to be as devout as they were, he got them to tell him exactly when the birth-announcement star appeared. Then he told them the prophecy about Bethlehem, and said, "Go find this child. Leave no stone unturned. As soon as you find him, send word and I'll join you at once in your worship."

M ATTHEW 2:7-8

Herod, impressive and fearful to his contemporaries, looks merely ridiculous to us. His secret, lying intrigues are useless before the ingenuous, unarmed invasion of history in Jesus at Bethlehem.

Who, to you, is the most impressive person in current history?

I am so used to being intimidated by conspiratorial evil, God, that I lose touch with the reality that your will is done, that your kingdom comes, and that the rulers of this world have very little to say about it, one way or the other. All praise to your omnipotent grace, your eternal love. Amen.

The Place of the Child

Instructed by the king, they set off. Then the star appeared again, the same star they had seen in the eastern skies. It led them on until it hovered over the place of the child. They could hardly contain themselves: They were in the right place! They had arrived at the right time!

MATTHEW 2:9-10

The dogma of the astrologer is that stars are impersonal cosmic arrangements that determine personal fate; the gospel is that stars are in God's services to "mark seasons and days and years" (Genesis 1:14). This star signals not our fate, but our freedom.

Why were the magi glad?

"I look up at your macro-skies, dark and enormous, your handmade sky-jewelry, Moon and stars mounted in their settings. Then I look at my micro-self and wonder, Why do you bother with us? Why take a second look our way?" (Psalm 8:3-4). Amen.

Kneeled and Worshiped

They entered the house and saw the child in the arms of Mary, his mother. Overcome, they kneeled and worshiped him. Then they opened their luggage and presented gifts: gold, frankincense, myrrh.

MATTHEW 2:11

The first thing that wise people do in the presence of Jesus is worship: not congratulate themselves on having found him, not ask him questions, not attempt to get something from him, but offer up themselves to him.

How do you worship?

In your presence, Lord Jesus, I want my life to be changed from getting things, to giving of myself, so that I may grow into wholeness. Amen.

Warned in a Dream

In a dream, they were warned not to report back to Herod. So they worked out another route, left the territory without being seen, and returned to their own country.

MATTHEW 2:12

A meeting with Herod would have been highly dramatic, just the kind of encounter that journalists delight in covering. Yet there is to be no dissipation of the act of worship in satisfying a king's curiosity, but an immediate return to everyday living in "their own country."

What are some results of worship?

God, connect the deepening and centering of life that I experience in moments of worship with the routines and duties of my weekday hours so that all of life will be glorified by your presence. Amen.

Flee to Egypt

After the scholars were gone, God's angel showed up again in Joseph's dream and commanded, "Get up. Take the child and his mother and flee to Egypt. Stay until further notice. Herod is on the hunt for this child, and wants to kill him." Joseph obeyed. He got up, took the child and his mother under cover of darkness. They were out of town and well on their way by daylight. They lived in Egypt until Herod's death. This Egyptian exile fulfilled what Hosea had preached: "I called my son out of Egypt."

MATTHEW 2:13-15

Herod's threat, which seems so ominous, was scarcely more than a pretext for accomplishing God's will. The flight into Egypt, retracing the ancient route of redemption, was part of a finely wrought salvation history.

What associations does Egypt have for you?

Lord, I see that Herod is real enough: He opens scenes, he triggers sequences, but he doesn't cause anything. Evil can't. Only you, God, cause, and what you cause is salvation, through Jesus, my Lord and Savior. Amen.

Rachel Weeping

Herod, when he realized that the scholars had tricked him, flew into a rage. He commanded the murder of every little boy two years old and under who lived in Bethlehem and its surrounding hills. (He determined that age from information he'd gotten from the scholars.) That's when Jeremiah's sermon was fulfilled: "A sound was heard in Ramah, weeping and much lament. Rachel weeping for her children, Rachel refusing all solace, her children gone, dead and buried."

MATTHEW 2:16-18

The slaughtered children participated in the messianic birth pangs: Christ entered a world flailing in rebellion. Herod, in a tantrum, hysterically tried to hold on to his kingdom. The voice in Ramah reverberates in history's echo chambers and gets louder every year.

What is the worst crime you are aware of?

Dear God, so much weeping! Such a burden of lamentation! I will not gloss over the terrible pain and sorrow that comes from vanity and anger, but neither will I forget the final word of resurrection. Amen.

Herod Died

Later, when Herod died, God's angel appeared in a dream to Joseph in Egypt: "Up, take the child and his mother and return to Israel. All those out to murder the child are dead." Joseph obeyed. He got up, took the child and his mother, and reentered Israel. When he heard, though, that Archelaus had succeeded his father, Herod, as king in Judea, he was afraid to go there. But then Joseph was directed in a dream to go to the hills of Galilee. On arrival, he settled in the village of Nazareth. This move was a fulfillment of the prophetic words, "He shall be called a Nazarene."

MATTHEW 2:19-23

Jesus' life began with men seeking to kill him; it ended in a similar atmosphere of conspiracy and violence. But the violence and plotting were as ineffective at the beginning as at the end. The holy family entered the holy land. Salvation gathered to full expression in a nuclear family in a provincial land.

How many dreams has Joseph had?

I trace out of my memory, O God, stories that have been fashioned on this old road between Egypt and Israel: stories of Abraham, and of Joseph and Moses; stories of faith and blessing and salvation. Thank you for including me in the stories. Amen.

In the Desert . . . Preaching

While Jesus was living in the Galilean hills, John, called "the Baptizer," was preaching in the desert country of Judea. His message was simple and austere, like his desert surroundings: "Change your life. God's kingdom is here." John and his message were authorized by Isaiah's prophecy: "Thunder in the desert! Prepare for God's arrival! Make the road smooth and straight!"

MATTHEW 3:1-3

The ancient Judean desert was the site of John's Messiah-readiness preaching. Everything is stark in the desert: the life-and-death contrasts, the vividness of minute details, the absence of the super-fluous, the emptiness. "Shall we never permit our hands to be empty so we may grasp what only empty hands can grasp?"[4]

What does "at hand" mean?

In this moment of silence and emptiness, O God, I wait and listen. Purge my spirit of sloth and train it in alert, messianic expectation. "In the deserts of the heart let the healing fountains start."[5] Amen.

John

John dressed in a camel-hair habit tied at the waist by a leather strap. He lived on a diet of locusts and wild field honey. People poured out of Jerusalem, Judea, and the Jordanian countryside to hear and see him in action. There at the Jordan River those who came to confess their sins were baptized into a changed life.

MATTHEW 3:4-6

John's food and clothing defied fashion. He found his identity not among market-oriented contemporaries, but among God-oriented prophets. John's single-mindedness proceeded from a deep immersion in the prophetic imagination and spirit.

Compare John with Elijah the Tishbite (2 Kings 1:8).

Lord, are there ways in which I can take the daily necessities of food and clothing and use them to complement and reinforce my relation with you? I will begin by giving thanks for them, in the name of Jesus Christ. Amen.

Slithering Down to the River

When John realized that a lot of Pharisees and Sadducees were showing up for a baptismal experience because it was becoming the popular thing to do, he exploded: "Brood of snakes! What do you think you're doing slithering down here to the river? Do you think a little water on your snakeskins is going to make any difference? It's your life that must change, not your skin! And don't think you can pull rank by claiming Abraham as father. Being a descendant of Abraham is neither here nor there. Descendants of Abraham are a dime a dozen. What counts is your life. Is it green and blossoming? Because if it's deadwood, it goes on the fire."

MATTHEW 3:7-10

Fleeing from wrath is not a gospel. The base lives and cowardly souls of the "brood of snakes" rushed to the Jordan for rescue. But John did not indulge their escapism; he called them to responsible action: "It's your life that must change, not your skin!"

What does repentance mean?

I am more comfortable, Father, with an image of you as a gentleman farmer, pruning an occasional branch and raking up a few leaves. But you go to the root. I submit myself to your surgery and hope in your salvation. Amen.

Ignite the Kingdom Life

"I'm baptizing you here in the river, turning your old life in for a kingdom life. The real action comes next: The main character in this drama—compared to him I'm a mere stagehand—will ignite the kingdom life within you, a fire within you, the Holy Spirit within you, changing you from the inside out. He's going to clean house—make a clean sweep of your lives. He'll place everything true in its proper place before God; everything false he'll put out with the trash to be burned."

MATTHEW 3:11-12

Two aspects of Jesus' baptism are described under the images of wind and fire. The wind brings something to us (the very breath of God), the fire takes something away from us (our worthless sins). Cleaning house is not always pleasant business. But the results are good. Who wants to be mixed with sin forever?

Has your life been swept clean?

I am grateful, God, that you take me with such seriousness and labor over me with such care. I now see myself sifted and cleansed by the wind of your Spirit, ready for use in your kingdom. Amen.

Baptized

Jesus then appeared, arriving at the Jordan River from Galilee. He wanted John to baptize him. John objected, "I'm the one who needs to be baptized, not *you*!" But Jesus insisted. "Do it. God's work, putting things right all these centuries, is coming together right now in this baptism." So John did it. The moment Jesus came up out of the baptismal waters, the skies opened up and he saw God's Spirit—it looked like a dove—descending and landing on him. And along with the Spirit, a voice: "This is my Son, chosen and marked by my love, delight of my life."

MATTHEW 3:13-17

Baptism personalizes the primordial Genesis beginnings. Just as the Spirit brooded birdlike over the ancient ocean deeps, so the Spirit descending "like a dove" is poised over the baptismal waters. The "it was good" of creation (Genesis 1:10) is completed by Christ as the "delight of my life."

What does your baptism mean?

I praise you, Almighty God, for speaking creative and eternity-shaping words over me, for showing me the goodness of your creation, and blessing me with the peace of your acceptance in Christ. Amen.

He Fasted Forty Days

Next Jesus was taken into the wild by the Spirit for the Test. The Devil was ready to give it. Jesus prayed for the Test by fasting forty days and forty nights. That left him, of course, in a state of extreme hunger . . .

MATTHEW 4:1-2

Moses was forty days on the mountain, in preparation for God's revelation; Elijah was forty days in the desert, in preparation for God's still small voice; Jesus was forty days in the wilderness, in preparation for the testing that would qualify him for the work of salvation.

What is the purpose of fasting?

What testing will you lead me into today, Lord? Prepare my heart so that I will hear your word and be led by your Spirit. Show me how to meet each test with energy and faith, trusting your victory in Christ. Amen.

Loaves of Bread

. . . which the Devil took advantage of in the first test: "Since you are God's Son, speak the word that will turn these stones into loaves of bread." Jesus answered by quoting Deuteronomy: "It takes more than bread to stay alive. It takes a steady stream of words from God's mouth."

MATTHEW 4:3-4

Bread, necessary though it is, is not primary: God is primary. Jesus will let nothing, not even necessary things, interfere with that primacy. Jesus will not use God to get what he wants; he submits himself to being what God wants.

How do you face this temptation?

Not what I want, but what you want, O God. Guard me from all temptations to use you to satisfy my earthly appetites. What I want most is to acquire new appetites, a hunger for righteousness, that will be satisfied by your word. Amen.

The Top of the Temple

For the second test the Devil took him to the Holy City. He sat him on top of the Temple and said, "Since you are God's Son, jump." The Devil goaded him by quoting Psalm 91: "He has placed you in the care of angels. They will catch you so that you won't so much as stub your toe on a stone." Jesus countered with another citation from Deuteronomy: "Don't you dare test the Lord your God."

MATTHEW 4:5-7

Miracles, attractive as they are, are not primary: God is primary. Jesus will not engage in a miracle-making that dazzles and entertains. Jesus will not use God as a means of showing off or attracting admirers. He has far more important things to do, working love and salvation.

How do you face this temptation?

Lord, protect me from being distracted by the sensational, from being diverted by the extraordinary. Keep me faithful in the daily round, attending to the common details of mercy and holiness. Amen.

The Peak of a Huge Mountain

For the third test, the Devil took him to the peak of a huge mountain. He gestured expansively, pointing out all the earth's kingdoms, how glorious they all were. Then he said, "They're yours—lock, stock, and barrel. Just go down on your knees and worship me, and they're yours." Jesus' refusal was curt: "Beat it, Satan!" He backed his rebuke with a third quotation from Deuteronomy: "Worship the Lord your God, and only him. Serve him with absolute single-heartedness."

MATTHEW 4:8-10

Power, important as it is, is not primary: God is primary. Jesus will not negotiate for power, even though he would be able to use the power benevolently. Goodness must not be compelled; love may not be coerced. The kingdom will "only come about through my Spirit" (Zechariah 4:6).

How do you face this temptation?

Lord, how often I face this temptation, the temptation to make people be good, to force them into the ways of righteousness. I always know so well what is good for others! Forgive me, Father, and give me the quiet, determined patience to love in mercy, to wait in hope. Amen.

Jesus Started Preaching

The Test was over. The Devil left. And in his place, angels! Angels came and took care of Jesus' needs. When Jesus got word that John had been arrested, he returned to Galilee. He moved from his hometown, Nazareth, to the lakeside village Capernaum, nestled at the base of the Zebulun and Naphtali hills. This move completed Isaiah's sermon: "Land of Zebulun, land of Naphtali, road to the sea, over Jordan, Galilee, crossroads for the nations. People sitting out their lives in the dark saw a huge light; sitting in that dark, dark country of death, they watched the sun come up." This Isaiah-prophesied sermon came to life in Galilee the moment Jesus started preaching. He picked up where John left off: "Change your life. God's kingdom is here."

MATTHEW 4:11-17

Thoroughly prepared by the temptations, Jesus began his ministry. Isaiah provided the text, Capernaum the pulpit. The message called everyone to alert response: God was at hand doing the work of making his will a present reality in salvation.

Compare Jesus' sermon with John the Baptist's (in Matthew 3).

What power, God, in these words! What life-changing truth, what mercy-releasing grace. I live in your presence, not in the hope of your presence; I participate in what is happening even now, not in what I wish would happen. Amen.

As He Walked by the Lake

Walking along the beach of Lake Galilee, Jesus saw two brothers: Simon (later called Peter) and Andrew. They were fishing, throwing their nets into the lake. It was their regular work. Jesus said to them, "Come with me. I'll make a new kind of fisherman out of you. I'll show you how to catch men and women instead of perch and bass." They didn't ask questions, but simply dropped their nets and followed. A short distance down the beach they came upon another pair of brothers, James and John, Zebedee's sons. These two were sitting in a boat with their father, Zebedee, mending their fishnets. Jesus made the same offer to them, and they were just as quick to follow, abandoning boat and father.

MATTHEW 4:18-22

Jesus began his work along Lake Galilee, not at the Jerusalem Temple. The world of common work, not the world of religious ritual, was where discipleship started. And fishermen, not priests, were the first disciples. Jesus comes to us, where we are, and initiates the work of kingdom-making.

From what does Jesus call you?

As you speak your commands to me, O Christ, complete your will in me. Convert me from a way of life bound to things to a life related to persons. The nets have absorbed my attention long enough; lead me into your way of being human. Amen.

On a Hillside

When Jesus saw his ministry drawing huge crowds, he climbed a hillside. Those who were apprenticed to him, the committed, climbed with him. Arriving at a quiet place, he sat down and taught his climbing companions. This is what he said . . .

MATTHEW 5:1-2

Surrounded by new disciples, Jesus began the teaching that would train them in the new life, which is God's kingdom. No words rival these in importance or power.

What do you know about the Sermon on the Mount?

My hope, Lord, as I attend to your teaching, is that I will be formed into your likeness, not just informed about what you once spoke to your disciples. I want to be thoroughly taught by you so that I can thoroughly live for you. Amen.

At the End of Your Rope

"You're blessed when you're at the end of your rope. With less of you there is more of God and his rule."

MATTHEW 5:3

Self-made and self-sufficient people live in a fantasy world, empty of the reality of God. In contrast, the poor in spirit are deeply aware of being God-made and God-sufficient: Everything derives from the goodness of God, and everything depends on the grace of God.

What does poor in spirit mean to you?

I empty my life, God, of all god-substitutes and all idol-alternatives. I have nothing so that I can receive everything. A life rich in wonder and blessing. Amen.

Lost What Is Most Dear

"You're blessed when you feel you've lost what is most dear to you. Only then can you be embraced by the One most dear to you."

MATTHEW 5:4

The willingness to respond to pain, to misfortune, to suffering, enables us to participate in the divine compassion that changes damnation to redemption. Sorrow does not get stuck in despair, but discovers comfort.

Whose sorrow do you share?

"O come and mourn with me a while; O come ye to the Savior's side; O come, together let us mourn: Jesus, our Lord, is crucified! . . . A broken heart, a fount of tears, ask, and they will not be denied; a broken heart love's cradle is: Jesus, our Lord, is crucified!"⁶ Amen.

The Content

"You're blessed when you're content with just who you are — no more, no less. That's the moment you find yourselves proud owners of everything that can't be bought."

MATTHEW 5:5

In a day when assertiveness is in vogue, contentment is likely to be dismissed out of hand. A precise understanding helps: It is not slack laziness but disciplined ambition; in place of riotous aggression, controlled obedience.

Who is the most content person you know?

Lord Jesus Christ, I will not deny my vitality or squelch my energy, but I will place them under your rule so that they will serve your purposes. I will not harness you to my requirements, but offer myself to yours. Amen.

A Good Appetite

"You're blessed when you've worked up a good appetite for God. He's food and drink in the best meal you'll ever eat."

Righteousness is food and drink for the whole person. It is never listed among the basic dietary items in the nutrition textbooks, but it is more important than any of them.

How do you express your appetite for God?

I hunger and thirst after your righteousness, dear God. Feed me on the bread of heaven, quench my thirst with the cup of blessing. Daily I will dine at your table, with Jesus as my host. Amen.

Care-Full

"You're blessed when you care. At the moment of being 'care-full,' you find yourselves cared for."

MATTHEW 5:7

God responds to our misfortunes, our ignorances, our failures, and our disobediences in ways that draw us close to him and save us from our trouble. Mercy. It is the opposite of the harsh condemnation that rejects. Because God does it, we can do it.

Who has treated you with unexpected care?

God, even as I have been accepted by you in mercy, help me to accept others—not condemning, not rejecting, not scolding, but sharing the promises of salvation through the mercies of Jesus Christ. Amen.

Your Mind and Heart Put Right

"You're blessed when you get your inside world—your mind and heart—put right. Then you can see God in the outside world."

MATTHEW 5:8

Dilettantes shop for God as they would for a new pair of shoes. Their purposes vacillate, and they live distracted. But simple intention is the way to comprehension and fellowship. "Purity of heart is to will one thing."[7]

What distracts you from God?

I have a difficult time, God, silencing the competing voices, shutting out the seductive images. I want you, but I want a lot of other things, too. "Put me together, one heart and mind; then, undivided, I'll worship in joyful fear" (Psalm 86:11). Amen.

Cooperate Not Compete

"You're blessed when you can show people how to cooperate instead of compete or fight. That's when you discover who you really are, and your place in God's family."

MATTHEW 5:9

Life in God's kingdom is not a competitive survival of the fittest. The prize does not go to the strongest and the swiftest. Jesus teaches us how to make peace with our neighbors, evoking the best in them, not destroy them as dangerous rivals.

Are you better at competition or cooperation?

Show me how to use my life, Jesus, in ways that will make others better, not get the better of them. I will no longer look at others as competitors for your favor, but as companions in your life of peacemaking. Amen.

Persecuted

"You're blessed when your commitment to God provokes persecution. The persecution drives you even deeper into God's kingdom."

MATTHEW 5:10

Lest we think that the peacemakers of verse 9 are bland, gray-flannel conformists who are afraid to rock the boat, Jesus defines our righteousness as that which frequently provokes opposition in a world whose values are called into question.

Who doesn't approve of your life in Christ?

When the storms of opposition come, dear Christ, help me to stand my ground and not hold back and instead throw myself into the work of the Master (see 1 Corinthians 15:58). Root me in righteousness so that my growth is impervious to popular dissent and always faithful to you. Amen.

Be Glad and Give a Cheer

"Not only that—count yourselves blessed every time people put you down or throw you out or speak lies about you to discredit me. What it means is that the truth is too close for comfort and they are uncomfortable. You can be glad when that happens—give a cheer, even!—for though they don't like it, *I* do! And all heaven applauds. And know that you are in good company. My prophets and witnesses have always gotten into this kind of trouble."

MATTHEW 5:11-12

If we take the offensive against our opposition, we are liable to harshness and bluster; if we get on the defensive, we lose initiative and appear timid and unsure. When we dance our faith, the enemy is disarmed and drawn into the celebration. Leaping joy is the sanity of blessing in a lunatic society.

What do you have cause to rejoice in?

Lord God, I will not use the world's weapons to fight your battles, and I will not be backed into a corner by those who scorn your love. Be with me as I celebrate my witness in joy and announce my confidence with gladness, for Jesus' sake. Amen.

Salt

"Let me tell you why you are here. You're here to be salt-seasoning that brings out the God-flavors of this earth. If you lose your saltiness, how will people taste godliness? You've lost your usefulness and will end up in the garbage."

MATTHEW 5:13

Minuscule and insignificant as individual Christians are, we are God's way of preserving society, of sharpening the taste buds of civilization. Our usefulness is not in what we do, but in what we are by God's grace.

What are the main uses of salt in your life?

Father, I keep thinking I have to rush out and do something; you keep calling me back to be someone. Use this life that you have created and redeemed to preserve and enhance those among whom I live today. Amen.

Light

"Here's another way to put it: You're here to be light, bringing out the God-colors in the world. God is not a secret to be kept. We're going public with this, as public as a city on a hill. If I make you light-bearers, you don't think I'm going to hide you under a bucket, do you? I'm putting you on a light stand. Now that I've put you there on a hilltop, on a light stand—shine!"

MATTHEW 5:14-15

Salt is a powerful, hidden influence; light is a blazing public illumination. Christian disciples are not only a behind-the-scenes influence, but also an out-in-the-open enlightenment.

What are the main uses of light in your life?

You, Lord, the light of the world, be light in me so that my life shows the clarity and warmth of your salvation. With your light I would not darken anyone's path by the shadows of my doubts or the gloom of my unbelief. Amen.

Open House

"Keep open house; be generous with your lives. By opening up to others, you'll prompt people to open up with God, this generous Father in heaven."

MATTHEW 5:16

Good works are an important means of witness; but they are also extremely susceptible to pride. Jesus can teach us how to use good works as glorifications of God and not simply as advertisements of ourselves.

What are some ways you can be generous with your life?

"So let our lips and lives express the holy gospel we profess; so let our works and virtues shine, to prove the doctrine all divine. Thus shall we best proclaim abroad the honors of our Savior God, when His salvation reigns within, and grace subdues the power of sin."[8] Amen.

Complete

"Don't suppose for a minute that I have come to demolish the Scriptures—either God's Law or the Prophets. I'm not here to demolish but to complete. I am going to put it all together, pull it all together in a vast panorama. God's Law is more real and lasting than the stars in the sky and the ground at your feet. Long after stars burn out and earth wears out, God's Law will be alive and working. Trivialize even the smallest item in God's Law and you will only have trivialized yourself. But take it seriously, show the way for others, and you will find honor in the kingdom. Unless you do far better than the Pharisees in the matters of right living, you won't know the first thing about entering the kingdom."

MATTHEW 5:17-20

No detail in the Law and the prophets was corrupt or obsolete. But much of it was empty. Sin cracks had appeared, and the vitality had leaked out. But Jesus does not therefore discard them—completion is the gospel program.

How does Jesus complete the Law and the prophets?

I see, Father, that there is nothing that you once used that cannot be used again. Lead me into the eternal meanings of your ancient words so that I may live in a present obedience, Christ living in me. Amen.

Far Better

"Unless you do far better than the Pharisees in the matters of right living, you won't know the first thing about entering the kingdom."

MATTHEW 5:20

Religion that is a matter of careful, moral calculation is all wrong. The gospel requires a leap of faith. Christ does not counsel a safe, manageable morality that anyone can learn in ten easy lessons, but a reckless adventurous life commitment.

What was the righteousness of the scribes?

I do not want to be a religious bookkeeper, Lord, but a faith explorer, ready to take risks without counting the cost, ready to love without taking out insurance against suffering, ready to plunge into obedience without calculating my rewards. Amen.

If You Are Angry

"You're familiar with the command to the ancients, 'Do not murder.' I'm telling you that anyone who is so much as angry with a brother or sister is guilty of murder. Carelessly call a brother 'idiot!' and you just might find yourself hauled into court. Thoughtlessly yell 'stupid!' at a sister and you are on the brink of hellfire. The simple moral fact is that words kill. This is how I want you to conduct yourself in these matters. If you enter your place of worship and, about to make an offering, you suddenly remember a grudge a friend has against you, abandon your offering, leave immediately, go to this friend and make things right. Then and only then, come back and work things out with God. Or say you're out on the street and an old enemy accosts you. Don't lose a minute. Make the first move; make things right with him. After all, if you leave the first move to him, knowing his track record, you're likely to end up in court, maybe even jail. If that happens, you won't get out without a stiff fine."

MATTHEW 5:21-26

The old commandment was intended to protect relationships, not just prevent murders. Anger that treats another contemptuously is murderous. Feelings that divide persons are destructive. Obedience reduced to not doing something is half-obedience.

Why is anger dangerous?

Do I diminish others, reduce them, despise them, God? With your help and direction I will augment them, respect them, and exalt them. Amen.

Blind Your Right Eye

"You know the next commandment pretty well, too: 'Don't go to bed with another's spouse.' But don't think you've preserved your virtue simply by staying out of bed. Your *heart* can be corrupted by lust even quicker than your *body*. Those leering looks you think nobody notices—they also corrupt. Let's not pretend this is easier than it really is. If you want to live a morally pure life, here's what you have to do: You have to blind your right eye the moment you catch it in a lustful leer. You have to choose to live one-eyed or else be dumped on a moral trash pile. And you have to chop off your right hand the moment you notice it raised threateningly. Better a bloody stump than your entire being discarded for good in the dump."

MATTHEW 5:27-30

No spirit surgery is too costly and no self-discipline too exacting in our development as Christ's servants. Our sin-split personalities think one thing and do another, or do one thing and think another. Jesus trains us in a mastery over self that brings us into single-minded devotion.

Compare this with 2 Corinthians 10:3-6.

Help me, O Christ, to maintain a ruthless mastery over my pride and self-centeredness so that every part of my life may be coordinated in acts of love. Amen.

Divorce

"Remember the Scripture that says, 'Whoever divorces his wife, let him do it legally, giving her divorce papers and her legal rights'? Too many of you are using that as a cover for selfishness and whim, pretending to be righteous just because you are 'legal.' Please, no more pretending. If you divorce your wife, you're responsible for making her an adulteress (unless she has already made herself that by sexual promiscuity). And if you marry such a divorced adulteress, you're automatically an adulterer yourself. You can't use legal cover to mask a moral failure."

MATTHEW 5:31-32

The guardian commandment on love, designed to protect intimate personal relationships, in practice had become the occasion for casuistic legalism. Jesus returns our attention to people and what happens to them.

What is wrong with divorce?

God, I know that you give commandments as tools that express your love, share your grace, and communicate your will, not as formulas for making me righteous. Help me to use them your way. For Jesus' sake. Amen.

Don't Say Anything
You Don't Mean

"And don't say anything you don't mean. This counsel is embedded deep in our traditions. You only make things worse when you lay down a smoke screen of pious talk, saying, 'I'll pray for you,' and never doing it, or saying, 'God be with you,' and not meaning it. You don't make your words true by embellishing them with religious lace. In making your speech sound more religious, it becomes less true. Just say 'yes' and 'no.' When you manipulate words to get your own way, you go wrong."

MATTHEW 5:33-37

Elaborate incantations or vehement curses are alike futile. God cannot be manipulated by our use of language. Prayer, the opposite of swearing, is language put to the service of God. It is the simplest and purest speech there is.

What Scriptures does Jesus quote?

God, purge all pretense and affectation from my speech. I want all my words to be an offering in love, all my speech a servant of truth, in the ways that Jesus taught. Amen.

Love Your Enemies

"Here's another old saying that deserves a second look: 'Eye for eye, tooth for tooth.' Is that going to get us anywhere? Here's what I propose: 'Don't hit back at all.' If someone strikes you, stand there and take it. If someone drags you into court and sues for the shirt off your back, giftwrap your best coat and make a present of it. And if someone takes unfair advantage of you, use the occasion to practice the servant life. No more tit-for-tat stuff. Live generously. You're familiar with the old written law, 'Love your friend,' and its unwritten companion, 'Hate your enemy.' I'm challenging that. I'm telling you to love your enemies. Let them bring out the best in you, not the worst. When someone gives you a hard time, respond with the energies of prayer, for then you are working out of your true selves, your God-created selves. That is what God does. He gives his best—the sun to warm and the rain to nourish—to everyone, regardless: the good and bad, the nice and nasty. If all you do is love the lovable, do you expect a bonus? Anybody can do that. If you simply say hello to those who greet you, do you expect a medal? Any run-of-the-mill sinner does that."

MATTHEW 5:38-47

Jesus commands a daring and courageous initiative that closes the gap between offender and offended. Love is not a reward to be parceled out as a favor to friends; it is a tactic by which we share the best in us so that others have an opportunity to live at their best.

Name an enemy you will love.

Christ of compassion, for too long I have let my emotions and my preju-dices tell me who and how to love. No longer. I will go to school in your salvation and learn your way of love. Amen.

Live Out Your God-Created Identity

"In a word, what I'm saying is, *Grow up*. You're kingdom subjects. Now live like it. Live out your God-created identity. Live generously and graciously toward others, the way God lives toward you."

MATTHEW 5:48

When we abandon the way of knee-jerk ethics — mindlessly reacting to the words and actions of others — we are free to become what love and grace stimulate in us: a wholeness that will finally be perfect.

Compare this with Ephesians 4:15-16.

Fashion in me what is obedient, eternal God, what is trusting and loving. Deal with what is rebellious, wayward, and misguided. I submit myself to your potter's hand. Amen.

Trying to Be Good

"Be especially careful when you are trying to be good so that you don't make a performance out of it. It might be good theater, but the God who made you won't be applauding."

MATTHEW 6:1

The Christians who care only for God's approval live free of the tyranny of conformist pressures, relaxed under the steady direction of the God who loves us and gives himself for us. Those who try to please the world by their good behavior very quickly find themselves under the unkind surveillance of a thousand critics.

What behavior of yours is determined by what people think?

Make me indifferent, God, to the world's approval, but sensitive to yours. How easy it is to get enlisted in the piety parade! Keep me from pretense, from poses, from posturings. For Jesus' sake. Amen.

Behind the Scenes

"When you do something for someone else, don't call attention to yourself. You've seen them in action, I'm sure—'playactors' I call them—treating prayer meeting and street corner alike as a stage, acting compassionate as long as someone is watching, playing to the crowds. They get applause, true, but that's all they get. When you help someone out, don't think about how it looks. Just do it—quietly and unobtrusively. That is the way your God, who conceived you in love, working behind the scenes, helps you out."

MATTHEW 6:2-4

When what is supposed to give aid to poor bodies becomes a means of aggrandizing proud spirits, piety is turned on its head. Nothing spoils acts of mercy and gifts of charity more quickly than publicity.

How do you keep from calling attention to your giving?

Father in heaven, lead me to speak in kindness and act in mercy unobtrusively and faithfully, just as you worked quietly and persistently behind the scenes in Jesus. Amen.

Not a Theatrical Production

"And when you come before God, don't turn that into a theatrical production either. All these people making a regular show out of their prayers, hoping for stardom! Do you think God sits in a box seat?"

MATTHEW 6:5

Prayer that is used for any other purpose, no matter how lofty, than to personally converse with a personal God is a sham. It must never be used as a part of public relations. It must never be put to the services of creating a good image.

Why might someone be tempted to make a show out of his or her prayers?

Free my spirit, God, from self-consciousness and self-righteousness. Forgive me for confusing the outward and the inward. Let my prayers be spontaneously honest and personally passionate. Amen.

When You Pray

"Here's what I want you to do: Find a quiet, secluded place so you won't be tempted to role-play before God. Just be there as simply and honestly as you can manage. The focus will shift from you to God, and you will begin to sense his grace."

MATTHEW 6:6

A quiet, secluded place diminishes our tendencies to pose and strut; it also eliminates distractions. Prayer is a conversation with God in which authenticity of spirit and attentiveness of mind are essential.

How do you get privacy in prayer?

"Father, in Thy mysterious presence kneeling, fain would our souls feel all Thy kindling love; for we are weak, and need some deep revealing of trust and strength and calmness from above."[9] Amen.

Peddling Techniques

"The world is full of so-called prayer warriors who are prayer-ignorant. They're full of formulas and programs and advice, peddling techniques for getting what you want from God."

MATTHEW 6:7

"Knowledge of speech, but not of silence; knowledge of words, and ignorance of the Word."[10] We live in an age of mass communication and minimal communion. When we have a good listener, we do not have to talk either a lot or loudly. God is a good listener.

Do you ever pray using formulas and empty phrases?

Holy Spirit, make the connection between the words of my mouth and the meanings in my heart so that my words may never be without personal meaning and my spirit never be without a means of expression. Amen.

Knows What You Need

"Don't fall for that nonsense. This is your Father you are dealing with, and he knows better than you what you need."

MATTHEW 6:8

Prayer is not a job list assigned by us to God. Nor is it a transfer of information between earth and heaven. God knows our condition and our needs. Prayer, like the best conversations on earth, cultivates intimacy, nurtures obedience, and becomes a way of working with God.

If God knows what you need, why pray?

In my prayers, O God, I will not make speeches to you, but nurture a relationship with you. I want to express myself completely and listen to you devoutly, in Jesus' name and for his sake. Amen.

Pray Like This

"With a God like this loving you, you can pray very simply. Like this: 'Our Father in heaven, reveal who you are. Set the world right; do what's best — as above, so below. Keep us alive with three square meals. Keep us forgiven with you and forgiving others. Keep us safe from ourselves and the Devil. You're in charge! You can do anything you want! You're ablaze in beauty! Yes. Yes. Yes.'"

MATTHEW 6:9-13

The act of praying is no uncharted wilderness where we hack and forge our way. It is well traveled, with rich traditions and deep culture. Jesus' words are compass and map for finding our way to the deep interiors.

Why is this prayer important to you?

"O Thou, by whom we come to God, the Life, the Truth, the Way; the path of Prayer Thyself hath trod; Lord, teach us how to pray!"[11] Amen.

Father

"With a God like this loving you, you can pray very simply. Like this: 'Our Father in heaven, reveal who you are.'"

MATTHEW 6:9

"Our" is the operative word. We cannot come to God as if he were a private deity, a household god. He is no personal idol we manufacture to our specifications. In prayer God is not reduced to our requirements; we are expanded to the dimensions of his majesty.

Why is "Father" such an important name for God?

Our Father: reveal yourself to me not as I have imagined you and not as others have stereotyped you, but as you really are: creator of all that is, loving redeemer of all your people. Amen.

Reveal Who You Are

"With a God like this loving you, you can pray very simply. Like this: 'Our Father in heaven, reveal who you are.'"

MATTHEW 6:9

The word "God" comprises goodness and holiness and glory. But in everyday usage it is marred with superstition. People read into the word "God" fears and ignorance and blasphemy. The name needs cleansing and burnishing.

How does God reveal himself to you?

Reveal who you are: purge the words that name your presence, cleanse the images that fill my mind. Scrape the noun clean of rust and grime until "Jesus" and "Christ" say the clear truth about you, Father. Amen.

Set the World Right

"Set the world right; do what's best—as above, so below."

MATTHEW 6:10

Every political scheme devised by humans is flawed somewhere, corrupt finally. The task of ordering people's lives in harmony and in fairness eludes our competence. Meanwhile, there are people who are already being ruled in love and who experience in that rule God's goodness and fulfillment.

What does "as above, so below" mean?

Set the world right. Establish your principles of redemption in me and among all who kneel in your presence and confess your lordship. Inaugurate your rule, Lord Jesus, and make me a charter citizen. Amen.

Choosing God's Best

"Set the world right; do what's best—as above, so below."

MATTHEW 6:10

Our wills are given to us to exercise freely. We can assert them noisily and brashly, like Adam, in choosing what is beneath us and thereby being diminished; or we can choose, like Christ, the way of our creator and redeemer and learn a greater freedom in an expanding reality.

How does your will differ from God's will?

Do what's best—as above, so below: the will that freely elects redemption in your creation, the will that comprehends all things and everyone in a divine purpose, the will that frees my will from slavery to sin and puts it to work in righteousness. Amen.

Three Square Meals

"Keep us alive with three square meals."

MATTHEW 6:11

God created our bodily as well as our spiritual hungers, and will provide for their satisfaction. Prayer has as much to do with the necessities of this day's living as with the certainties of eternal life.

What physical needs will you pray for today?

Keep us alive with three square meals: I will not let my needs become anxieties but will submit them to your providence. Give, Lord, all that I need to live obediently and joyously. Amen.

Forgive

"Keep us forgiven with you and forgiving others."

MATTHEW 6:12

Apart from forgiveness each step we take is a link in the cause-and-effect sequence of sin and death. With forgiveness we travel from "strength to strength" by grace to life eternal. In the same way that bread is a basic need for the body, forgiveness is the basic need of the spirit.

Who can you forgive as you have been forgiven?

Keep us forgiven with you and forgiving others: I want each detail of my life to be a result not of the sins I commit, but of the mercy you pour out in Jesus. Don't, God, ignore me, indulge me, or reject me. Forgive me. Amen.

Safe

"Keep us safe from ourselves and the Devil."

MATTHEW 6:13

Christians are not moral giants, flexing our muscles and displaying our trophies before the world as evidence of superior spirituality. We are in a battle that very often threatens to overwhelm us, and we need help.

What do you need to be kept safe from?

Keep us safe from ourselves and the Devil: I thank you, God, that you are not coolly manipulating me, puppet-like, on a string; but that you are with me, on my side in this war for eternal life, and that you will bring the victory. Amen.

Yes

"You're in charge! You can do anything you want! You're ablaze in beauty! Yes. Yes. Yes."

MATTHEW 6:13

In these closing statements to the Lord's Prayer, Jesus summarizes the languge spoken in God's kingdom, voiced with energy given by God's power, and however stuttering, resplendent with God's glory.

How does the Lord's Prayer help you to pray?

You're in charge! You can do anything you want! You're ablaze in beauty! All that you are, O God, evokes and shapes my prayers to you. Keep me in the company of all who are struggling to master this tongue. Help me to be articulate in this great language. Amen.

Forgiveness

"In prayer there is a connection between what God does and what you do. You can't get forgiveness from God, for instance, without also forgiving others. If you refuse to do your part, you cut yourself off from God's part."

MATTHEW 6:14-15

God's work includes our neighbors, and we must join him in it if we are to continue in his ways. We are always trying to reduce God's work to something exclusive and private, but he will not permit it.

Whom will you forgive today?

At first, Lord, these words look like a posted warning, but now I see in them a way of promise—your words of forgiveness spill out into the world through my acts of forgiveness. Thank you for letting me share in your great and creative work of forgiving. Amen.

Don't Make a Production

"When you practice some appetite-denying discipline to better concentrate on God, don't make a production out of it. It might turn you into a small-time celebrity but it won't make you a saint. If you 'go into training' inwardly, act normal outwardly. Shampoo and comb your hair, brush your teeth, wash your face. God doesn't require attention-getting devices. He won't overlook what you are doing; he'll reward you well."

MATTHEW 6:16-18

Routines dull perceptions. The purpose of a discipline such as fasting is to interrupt the routines that cushion us from the foundational realities and so sharpen our awareness of the eternal essentials.

Will you choose a day, or a meal, to fast this week?

Lord God, I let too many things distract and divert me from paying attention to you. Train me in the simplifications that will put me in touch with what matters most—your love, your salvation, your grace. Amen.

Treasure

"Don't hoard treasure down here where it gets eaten by moths and corroded by rust or—worse!—stolen by burglars. Stockpile treasure in heaven, where it's safe from moth and rust and burglars. It's obvious, isn't it? The place where your treasure is, is the place you will most want to be, and end up being."

MATTHEW 6:19-21

God has nothing against treasure; his concern is about its location. The location of our treasure, that upon which we expend energy and fix hopes, determines the direction of our goals and the shape of our behavior.

What do you value most?

Father, I put all my wealth, my investments, my possessions in trust. You are my future and my confidence. Cure me of the possessiveness that holds tightly and will not let go. Amen.

Open Your Eyes Wide

"Your eyes are windows into your body. If you open your eyes wide in wonder and belief, your body fills up with light. If you live squinty-eyed in greed and distrust, your body is a dank cellar. If you pull blinds on your windows, what a dark life you will have!"

MATTHEW 6:22-23

Our eyes are remarkable and accurate signs of our inner spiritual health. They narrow into slits when we hate, envy, and scheme. They open wide in wonder when we live in adoration and generosity.

What obstructs your vision of God?

God, your world is so full of people to love and things to admire. Keep my eyes wide open to receive all the sensations of color and form in your creation and to love everything and everyone I see in Jesus' name. Amen.

Two Gods

"You can't worship two gods at once. Loving one god, you'll end up hating the other. Adoration of one feeds contempt for the other. You can't worship God and Money both."

MATTHEW 6:24

Faith is not an amalgam of all the bits and pieces of "religion" that are deposited in the delta of the soul. The Christian is not a collection bin for every religious emotion that passes through the nervous system. Christian faith is choice and service — choosing Christ as Savior and serving him as Lord.

How would you serve "money"?

I know, God, that I cannot trust you as just another item in the religious stew I keep simmering on the back burner of my life. Master me absolutely so that I may serve you in body, mind, and spirit, as I now attend to your word of creation and command in Jesus Christ. Amen.

Don't Fuss

"If you decide for God, living a life of God-worship, it follows that you don't fuss about what's on the table at mealtimes or whether the clothes in your closet are in fashion. There is far more to your life than the food you put in your stomach, more to your outer appearance than the clothes you hang on your body. Look at the birds, free and unfettered, not tied down to a job description, careless in the care of God. And you count far more to him than birds."

MATTHEW 6:25-26

Survival needs, important as they are, must not be allowed to define or dominate us. We are created for something far more complex and profound than food and drink and clothing. God's love, care, and providence are the wide world in which we learn to live easily and exuberantly.

What anxiety will you turn over to God?

Father in heaven, forgetful of my high calling in Christ, I find myself flattened out on an economic plain, living from hand to mouth with a mean, survival mentality. Awaken the desire to live by your will, as your child, in your love. Amen.

So Much as an Inch?

"Has anyone by fussing in front of the mirror ever gotten taller by so much as an inch?"

MATTHEW 6:27

Anxiety burns up enormous amounts of energy, wastefully and inefficiently. It produces nothing. It is the opposite of faith, which requires only plain attentiveness to God and simple responses to his will—and moves mountains.

Compare anxiety with the faith described in Hebrews 11:1.

Lord Jesus Christ, you have so richly and extravagantly provided me with meaning and purpose and beauty and goodness—what more do I want? Help me not to be anxious but to find contentment and put my trust in you. Amen.

Look at the Wildflowers

"Has anyone by fussing in front of the mirror ever gotten taller by so much as an inch? All this time and money wasted on fashion—do you think it makes that much difference? Instead of looking at the fashions, walk out into the fields and look at the wildflowers. They never primp or shop, but have you ever seen color and design quite like it? The ten best-dressed men and women in the country look shabby alongside them. If God gives such attention to the appearance of wildflowers—most of which are never even seen—don't you think he'll attend to you, take pride in you, do his best for you?"

MATTHEW 6:27-30

Anxious preoccupation with the needs and wants of daily living distract us from God, who is already present in each detail to help, strengthen, provide, and redeem by his love.

Compare this passage to Matthew 8:26; 14:31; and 16:8.

Dear Christ, I set aside right now my nervous concern for what I must do; I center my thoughts on what you are doing in me and in the world. I want to trade in my anxieties for your gift of faith. Amen.

You Know How God Works

"What I'm trying to do here is to get you to relax, to not be so preoccupied with *getting*, so you can respond to God's *giving*. People who don't know God and the way he works fuss over these things, but you know both God and how he works."

MATTHEW 6:31-32

Faith breathes a confidence that God knows our needs better than we do and provides for their fulfillment. The frantic doubt that God may have forgotten about us, the panicky suspicion that God may have decided against us—all that is excluded by faith.

What are you most sure of in God?

For your uninterrupted mercy, O God, for the constant surveillance of your provident eye, for the steady assistance of your strong arm, for the persistent invitational knocking at the door of my life, for these I give thanks. Amen.

Steep Your Life

"Steep your life in God-reality, God-initiative, God-provisions. Don't worry about missing out. You'll find all your everyday human concerns will be met."

MATTHEW 6:33

Our priorities should be clear by now: We are made by God, for God; therefore the meaning and fulfillment of our lives must take place in the country of grace. What he says and what he does, and how we respond and how we obey, are the center realities of our lives.

What evidence is there in your life that you are pursuing the things of God?

"Be still, my soul: the Lord is on thy side; bear patiently the cross of grief or pain; leave to thy God to order and provide; in every change He faithful will remain. Be still, my soul: thy best, thy heavenly Friend through thorny ways leads to a joyful end."[12] Amen.

Don't Worry

"Steep your life in God-reality, God-initiative, God-provisions. Don't worry about missing out. You'll find all your everyday human concerns will be met. Give your entire attention to what God is doing right now, and don't get worked up about what may or may not happen tomorrow. God will help you deal with whatever hard things come up when the time comes."

MATTHEW 6:33-34

If we are in control of what happens to us and in charge of our own well-being, we do well to be perpetually vigilant against evil and on constant alert for the lucky break. But if God is in control, if his kingdom is already a reality, we are separated from such debilitating anxieties.

What are you giving your attention to?

My God and King: In the course of this day, as I am presented with choices to make and paths to follow, give me the wise courage to decide to live in your reality, where I will experience your power and glory in Jesus Christ. Amen.

Don't Criticize

"Don't pick on people, jump on their failures, criticize their faults—unless, of course, you want the same treatment. That critical spirit has a way of boomeranging."

MATTHEW 7:1-2

When we criticize others—evaluate their worthlessness, their lack of virtue, their practice of vice—we waste the moral energies that were given to us for use in the work of compassion. Examining others with an eye to spotting their defects is self-destructive.

Whom are you tempted to judge?

I find, by your word, O God, that I am utterly incompetent to criticize others. I have only meager information about them; I only vaguely understand your purposes in them. Instead of pronouncing judgments on them, I will work and pray for them, in Jesus' name. Amen.

The Smudge / The Sneer

"It's easy to see a smudge on your neighbor's face and be oblivious to the ugly sneer on your own. Do you have the nerve to say, 'Let me wash your face for you,' when your own face is distorted by contempt? It's this whole traveling road-show mentality all over again, playing a holier-than-thou part instead of just living your part. Wipe that ugly sneer off your own face, and you might be fit to offer a washcloth to your neighbor."

MATTHEW 7:3-5

Not until we refuse to indulge our curiosity about what is wrong with others are we free to take a genuine interest in them as people loved by God to whom we may become witnesses in truth and companions in faith. Too many times we confuse religious gossip with spiritual concern.

Whom are you judging instead of loving?

Lord, bring me to the place where my interest is not in condemning sin in others, but in confessing it in myself. I find it much easier to mount an indignant assault on everyone else's sins than to repent and be cleansed of my own. Amen.

Don't Be Flip with the Sacred

"Don't be flip with the sacred. Banter and silliness give no honor to God. Don't reduce holy mysteries to slogans. In trying to be relevant, you're only being cute and inviting sacrilege."

MATTHEW 7:6

Our Lord leads us in knowing when to speak and act, just as he teaches us what is to be done and spoken. Timing is important in witnessing and helping, teaching and preaching. "Readiness is all."[13]

What good deeds have you done in the wrong place?

Holy Spirit, give me the gift of discerning hearts and being sensitive to needs, so that as I share the truth and goodness of my Lord, I may not provoke rejection by my rudeness nor encourage irreverence by my ignorance. For Jesus' sake. Amen.

Ask

"Don't bargain with God. Be direct. Ask for what you need."

MATTHEW 7:7

When we ask we admit our inadequacy and confess God's sufficiency. Asking is the basic prayer. In such prayer, connections are soldered between our brokenness and his wholeness.

What will you ask from God today?

Great God, consummate all my desires in your love; complete all my wants in your grace. Thank you for the invitation and the promise: the invitation to put all my needs before you, the promise that you will meet them in wisdom and peace. Amen.

Do It for Them

"Here is a simple, rule-of-thumb guide for behavior: Ask yourself what you want people to do for you, then grab the initiative and do it for *them*. Add up God's Law and Prophets and this is what you get."

MATTHEW 7:12

The most remarkable thing about this summary sentence on behavior is not in the words themselves but in the life-commentary that Jesus provided. This is what he did. He converted all morality from wish to reality, from ideal to actuality. And what he did he enables us to do.

How can you use this golden rule in a specific action?

"So let our lips and lives express the holy gospel we profess; so let our works and virtues shine, to prove the doctrine all divine. Thus shall we best proclaim abroad the honors of our Savior God, when His salvation reigns within, and grace subdues the power of sin."[14] Amen.

Total Attention Required

"Don't look for shortcuts to God. The market is flooded with surefire, easygoing formulas for a successful life that can be practiced in your spare time. Don't fall for that stuff, even though crowds of people do. The way to life—to God!—is vigorous and requires total attention."

MATTHEW 7:13-14

Faith is not an accumulation of vague impulses that tend, generally, toward the good, nor is it the nurture of obscure emotions of piety; it is choosing to walk through a particular gate ("I am the Gate" [John 10:7]) and down a definite road ("I am the Road" [John 14:6]).

What do you find difficult or demanding about God's way to life?

Lord Jesus, you are my way and my truth and my life. Lead me through the place of concentrated decision into the country of expansive blessings. Amen.

Be Wary of False Preachers

"Be wary of false preachers who smile a lot, dripping with practiced sincerity."

MATTHEW 7:15

Christian charity must not be confused with pious gullibility that puts up with fraud and nonsense in its leaders. Religious claims are the easiest to make, but the hardest to document. Prophetic mantles easily assumed must be painstakingly verified.

How do you exercise caution toward religious leaders?

Give me, Lord, the gift of discernment so that I may not be led astray by those who prey upon my faith, so that I may not be exploited by those who would profit from my devotion. For Jesus' sake. Amen.

Bad Apples

"Chances are they are out to rip you off some way or other. Don't be impressed with charisma; look for character. Who preachers *are* is the main thing, not what they say. A genuine leader will never exploit your emotions or your pocketbook. These diseased trees with their bad apples are going to be chopped down and burned."

MATTHEW 7:16-20

In evaluating religious leadership, it is far more useful to observe how a person treats his dog than to ask him for his opinions on God. A person's "fruit" is not success anecdotes or upward-swinging statistical curves but instances in which it is obvious that inward belief has metamorphosed into behavior.

What fruit do you see in your spiritual leaders?

Father, I don't want to be uncritically naive toward someone just because he or she is called pastor, or preacher, or evangelist; but neither do I want to develop a cynical skepticism toward anyone who is in the spotlight. Show me the middle way of alert obedience in and through Jesus Christ. Amen.

Master, Master

"Knowing the correct password—saying 'Master, Master,' for instance—isn't going to get you anywhere with me. What is required is serious obedience—*doing* what my Father wills. I can see it now—at the Final Judgment thousands strutting up to me and saying, 'Master, we preached the Message, we bashed the demons, our God-sponsored projects had everyone talking.' And do you know what I am going to say? 'You missed the boat. All you did was use me to make yourselves important. You don't impress me one bit. You're out of here.'"

MATTHEW 7:21-23

Name-dropping works the same way in spiritual things as it does in earthly things—it gives the impression of intimacy when there is only the flimsiest of relationships. Using the name will get us nowhere if we are unrelated to the person we name.

Are you a religious name-dropper?

Lord Christ, when I use your name, keep me honest so that I am expressing a relationship with you and engaging in a response to your will. I want my whole life, not just my mouth, to speak your name. Amen.

On Solid Rock

"These words I speak to you are not incidental additions to your life, homeowner improvements to your standard of living. They are foundational words, words to build a life on. If you work these words into your life, you are like a smart carpenter who built his house on solid rock. Rain poured down, the river flooded, a tornado hit — but nothing moved that house. It was fixed to the rock. But if you just use my words in Bible studies and don't work them into your life, you are like a stupid carpenter who built his house on the sandy beach. When a storm rolled in and the waves came up, it collapsed like a house of cards."

MATTHEW 7:24-27

Visible behavior is built on invisible truth. Jesus provides the commands that, as we obey them, are solid, foundational underpinnings for eternal life.

What are some items in your life foundation?

All praise to you, O God, for giving me such weighty, sure, foundation-making commands. Thank you for giving me the desire to respond to them in obedient belief. Give me daily directions for building upon Christ the rock. Amen.

The Best Teaching

When Jesus concluded his address, the crowd burst into applause. They had never heard teaching like this. It was apparent that he was living everything he was saying—quite a contrast to their religion teachers! This was the best teaching they had ever heard.

MATTHEW 7:28-29

The world is so full of people who attempt to shock, startle, and surprise us that we finally become blasé. Then our Lord comes along and speaks the truth simply and truly. The sheer authenticity and naked reality of it shakes us out of our ennui.

What is most astonishing to you in Jesus' words?

"My hope is built on nothing less than Jesus' blood and righteousness; I dare not trust the sweetest frame, but wholly lean on Jesus' name. On Christ, the solid rock, I stand; all other ground is sinking sand."[15] Amen.

Master, If You Want To

Jesus came down the mountain with the cheers of the crowd still ringing in his ears. Then a leper appeared and went to his knees before Jesus, praying, "Master, if you want to, you can heal my body." Jesus reached out and touched him, saying, "I want to. Be clean." Then and there, all signs of the leprosy were gone. Jesus said, "Don't talk about this all over town. Just quietly present your healed body to the priest, along with the appropriate expressions of thanks to God. Your cleansed and grateful life, not your words, will bear witness to what I have done."

MATTHEW 8:1-4

The leper is the needy person in extremis: cut off, lonely, shunned. But no needy condition is so extreme or so absolute that we are consigned to despair. There is hope in God. The approach, timid and tentative — "if you want to" — unexpectedly finds a bold and positive desire to save: "I want to."

What was so bad about being a leper?

I want cleansing, dear Christ, quite as much as that leper. But in your way; what you will. I want my life to be shaped not by my demands, but by the sure and mysterious movement of your grace. Amen.

Just Give the Order

As Jesus entered the village of Capernaum, a Roman captain came up in a panic and said, "Master, my servant is sick. He can't walk. He's in terrible pain." Jesus said, "I'll come and heal him." "Oh, no," said the captain. "I don't want to put you to all that trouble. Just give the order and my servant will be fine. I'm a man who takes orders and gives orders. I tell one soldier, 'Go,' and he goes; to another, 'Come,' and he comes; to my slave, 'Do this,' and he does it." Taken aback, Jesus said, "I've yet to come across this kind of simple trust in Israel, the very people who are supposed to know all about God and how he works. This man is the vanguard of many outsiders who will soon be coming from all directions—streaming in from the east, pouring in from the west, sitting down at God's kingdom banquet alongside Abraham, Isaac, and Jacob. Then those who grew up 'in the faith' but had no faith will find themselves out in the cold, outsiders to grace and wondering what happened." Then Jesus turned to the captain and said, "Go. What you believed could happen has happened." At that moment his servant became well.

MATTHEW 8:5-13

The captain did what he knew best; he used everyday experience (his military training) to gain access to the operations of God. Faith, in this case, is not an extraordinary leap into the unknown, but a commonplace step into what is clear and present in Jesus.

Whom do you want Jesus to help?

Christ, there are so many paralyzed people around, so many servant-children helpless apart from you. Help them. I can't help them; I only run to you and announce the "terrible pain" to which you are neither impotent nor indifferent. Amen.

Ready to Rough It?

By this time they were in front of Peter's house. On entering, Jesus found Peter's mother-in-law sick in bed, burning up with fever. He touched her hand and the fever was gone. No sooner was she up on her feet than she was fixing dinner for him. That evening a lot of demon-afflicted people were brought to him. He relieved the inwardly tormented. He cured the bodily ill. He fulfilled Isaiah's well-known sermon: "He took our illnesses, he carried our diseases." When Jesus saw that a curious crowd was growing by the minute, he told his disciples to get him out of there to the other side of the lake. As they left, a religion scholar asked if he could go along. "I'll go with you, wherever," he said. Jesus was curt: "Are you ready to rough it? We're not staying in the best inns, you know." Another follower said, "Master, excuse me for a couple of days, please. I have my father's funeral to take care of." Jesus refused. "First things first. Your business is life, not death. Follow me. Pursue life."

MATTHEW 8:14-22

Jesus responds to our desire for a closer walk with him by reading us the fine print of discipleship: a loss of creature comforts ("We're not staying in the best inns") and a setting aside of old priorities ("Your business is life, not death").

How does Christ change your values?

I want to go where you go, Jesus. I think I am willing to do anything. Then you confront me with where you are going and what you are doing, and I am not so sure. Give me, along with the desire to be with you, the courage to stay with you. Amen.

Faint-Hearts

Then he got in the boat, his disciples with him. The next thing they knew, they were in a severe storm. Waves were crashing into the boat—and he was sound asleep! They roused him, pleading, "Master, save us! We're going down!" Jesus reprimanded them. "Why are you such cowards, such faint-hearts?" Then he stood up and told the wind to be silent, the sea to quiet down: "Silence!" The sea became smooth as glass. The men rubbed their eyes, astonished. "What's going on here? Wind and sea come to heel at his command!"

MATTHEW 8:23-27

By this time these disciples should have known whom they were with, and what happened when they were with him. But they were more worried about the weather than they were trustful of their Savior.

Would you have been afraid?

My goal, Savior Christ, is to believe in you so deeply and thoroughly that my first response in every crisis is faith in what you will do, trust in how you will bless. But I have a long way to go. Lead me from my fearful midget-faith to mature adulthood. Amen.

Get Out and Don't Come Back

They landed in the country of the Gadarenes and were met by two madmen, victims of demons, coming out of the cemetery. The men had terrorized the region for so long that no one considered it safe to walk down that stretch of road anymore. Seeing Jesus, the madmen screamed out, "What business do you have giving us a hard time? You're the Son of God! You weren't supposed to show up here yet!" Off in the distance a herd of pigs was browsing and rooting. The evil spirits begged Jesus, "If you kick us out of these men, let us live in the pigs." Jesus said, "Go ahead, but get out of here!" Crazed, the pigs stampeded over a cliff into the sea and drowned. Scared to death, the swineherds bolted. They told everyone back in town what had happened to the madmen and the pigs. Those who heard about it were angry about the drowned pigs. A mob formed and demanded that Jesus get out and not come back.

MATTHEW 8:28-34

In Gadara, property was valued more highly than people. That two people were restored to sanity was a triviality compared to the loss of their pigs. They wanted nothing to do with Jesus if it meant they had more people to love and less property to hold.

What does Jesus do to your value system?

Where are my values, Lord Jesus? I pay lip service to the priorities of people, but I give an enormous amount of time and attention to things. Examine me carefully; if there is any possession that is making it impossible for me to love people and praise you for your work in them, show me how to get rid of it. Amen.

I Forgive Your Sins

Back in the boat, Jesus and the disciples recrossed the sea to Jesus' hometown. They were hardly out of the boat when some men carried a paraplegic on a stretcher and set him down in front of them. Jesus, impressed by their bold belief, said to the paraplegic, "Cheer up, son. I forgive your sins." Some religion scholars whispered, "Why, that's blasphemy!" Jesus knew what they were thinking, and said, "Why this gossipy whispering? Which do you think is simpler: to say, 'I forgive your sins,' or, 'Get up and walk'? Well, just so it's clear that I'm the Son of Man and authorized to do either, or both. . . ." At this he turned to the paraplegic and said, "Get up. Take your bed and go home." And the man did it. The crowd was awestruck, amazed and pleased that God had authorized Jesus to work among them this way.

MATTHEW 9:1-8

Everyone, both the man and his friends, thought his basic need was physical. How surprised they were to hear Jesus address the invisible spiritual need. Jesus got around to the physical, but he began with the man's heart.

What do you think of as your most pressing need?

God, I wish for and pray for many noble things that are secondary and peripheral. My agenda of petition lacks theology—I fail to see my life in relation primarily to you. Deal with my needs as you see them. Get to my center and save me. Amen.

Come Along with Me

Passing along, Jesus saw a man at his work collecting taxes. His name was Matthew. Jesus said, "Come along with me." Matthew stood up and followed him.

MATTHEW 9:9

God in Jesus addresses us by a personal name and with a personal command. He does not impersonally recruit us as workers or functionaries. When we respond, we move out of a life in which what we do or others do is the main thing and into a life where God is the controlling center.

What do you know about tax collectors?

"Follow, I would follow Thee, my Lord, follow every passing day. My tomorrows are all known to Thee, Thou wilt lead me all the way."[16] Amen.

Mercy, Not Religion

Later when Jesus was eating supper at Matthew's house with his close followers, a lot of disreputable characters came and joined them. When the Pharisees saw him keeping this kind of company, they had a fit, and lit into Jesus' followers. "What kind of example is this from your Teacher, acting cozy with crooks and riffraff?" Jesus, overhearing, shot back, "Who needs a doctor: the healthy or the sick? Go figure out what this Scripture means: 'I'm after mercy, not religion.' I'm here to invite outsiders, not coddle insiders."

MATTHEW 9:10-13

The key word here is *mercy*— the divine will and energy of helping the hurt and saving the lost. It is set in contrast to *religion*— the human attempt to arrange appearances so that they are pleasing to God.

How do Jesus' words change your outlook on life?

When I see things from your point of view, Lord Jesus, though everything is the same, everything is different. Life is lived in grateful response to your mercy, not in obsessive and fearful attempts to look good. I can relax. I can praise. I can live to your glory. Amen.

Cracked Bottles

A little later John's followers approached, asking, "Why is it that we and the Pharisees rigorously discipline body and spirit by fasting, but your followers don't." Jesus told them, "When you're celebrating a wedding, you don't skimp on the cake and wine. You feast. Later you may need to pull in your belt, but not now. No one throws cold water on a friendly bonfire. This is Kingdom Come!" He went on, "No one cuts up a fine silk scarf to patch old work clothes; you want fabrics that match. And you don't put your wine in cracked bottles."

MATTHEW 9:14-17

Fasting was, and is, a noble religious discipline. But fasting was not an end in itself to be gradually perfected through the centuries but rather preparation for a feast. And now the feast is served!

Do you ever confuse preparation with fulfillment?

Father in heaven, keep me flexible and responsive to your presence in my life so that I will be ready at any moment to stop what I am doing in getting ready for you and go with you in service or in praise, in witness or in celebration. Amen.

Daughter

As he finished saying this, a local official appeared, bowed politely, and said, "My daughter has just now died. If you come and touch her, she will live." Jesus got up and went with him, his disciples following along. Just then a woman who had hemorrhaged for twelve years slipped in from behind and lightly touched his robe. She was thinking to herself, "If I can just put a finger on his robe, I'll get well." Jesus turned—caught her at it. Then he reassured her: "Courage, daughter. You took a risk of faith, and now you're well." The woman was well from then on. By now they had arrived at the house of the town official, and pushed their way through the gossips looking for a story and the neighbors bringing in casseroles. Jesus was abrupt: "Clear out! This girl isn't dead. She's sleeping." They told him he didn't know what he was talking about. But when Jesus had gotten rid of the crowd, he went in, took the girl's hand, and pulled her to her feet—alive.

MATTHEW 9:18-25

The two daughters, the one twelve years old and the other twelve years sick, had their stories held together. The anonymous woman in the crowd was healed with the same attentive tenderness as the daughter of one of the most prominent men in town.

What comparisons and contrasts do you see between the two?

When, Lord, will I learn the grand and ever freshly documented truth—no one is beneath your attention, no person is beyond your help. Keep me from the sin of despair, always ready for your resurrection word. Amen.

Two Blind Men

As Jesus left the house, he was followed by two blind men crying out, "Mercy, Son of David! Mercy on us!" When Jesus got home, the blind men went in with him. Jesus said to them, "Do you really believe I can do this?" They said, "Why, yes, Master!" He touched their eyes and said, "Become what you believe." It happened. They saw. Then Jesus became very stern. "Don't let a soul know how this happened." But they were hardly out the door before they started blabbing it to everyone they met.

MATTHEW 9:27-31

The two blind men were typical of many: They enjoyed immensely the benefits of being with Jesus but blithely ignored his commands. As long as they needed help, they were all eagerness and attention; as soon as they got what they came for, they disregarded Jesus completely.

Why did the healed men disobey Jesus' command for silence?

Jesus Christ, I want to take your words to me just as seriously and personally as I do your acts for me. I need your help, but I also need your direction. Lead me from the faith that responds to your mercy into the faith that becomes obedient discipleship. Amen.

A Huge Harvest

Right after that, as the blind men were leaving, a man who had been struck speechless by an evil spirit was brought to Jesus. As soon as Jesus threw the evil tormenting spirit out, the man talked away just as if he'd been talking all his life. The people were up on their feet applauding: "There's never been anything like this is Israel!" The Pharisees were left sputtering, "Hocus pocus. It's nothing but hocus pocus. He's probably made a pact with the Devil." Then Jesus made a circuit of all the towns and villages. He taught in their meeting places, reported kingdom news, and healed their diseased bodies, healed their bruised and hurt lives. When he looked out over the crowds, his heart broke. So confused and aimless they were, like sheep with no shepherd. "What a huge harvest!" he said to his disciples. "How few workers! On your knees and pray for harvest hands!"

MATTHEW 9:32-38

To this point in the narrative, the emphasis has been on the ministry of Jesus. Now there is a transition as he enlists others in the work of compassion. Jesus not only helps us, he helps us to help others.

Where do you see a huge harvest?

"Come, labor on, who dares stand idle on the harvest plain while all around him waves the golden grain? And to each servant does the Master say, Go work today."[17] Amen.

Live Generously

The prayer was no sooner prayed than it was answered. Jesus called twelve of his followers and sent them into the ripe fields. He gave them power to kick out the evil spirits and to tenderly care for the bruised and hurt lives. . . . Jesus sent his twelve harvest hands out with this charge: "Don't begin by traveling to some far-off place to convert unbelievers. And don't try to be dramatic by tackling some public enemy. Go to the lost, confused people right here in the neighborhood. Tell them that the kingdom is here. Bring health to the sick. Raise the dead. Touch the untouchables. Kick out the demons. You have been treated generously, so live generously. Don't think you have to put on a fund-raising campaign before you start. You don't need a lot of equipment. *You* are the equipment, and all you need to keep that going is three meals a day. Travel light."

MATTHEW 10:1,5-10

We don't just receive Christ's ministry, we share it. Each Christian is a nexus for grace, an intersection of redemptive traffic. All the vigorous energies of joy (preaching), intelligence (teaching), and health (healing) spill out of our lives into the world.

What kind of ministry are you good at?

The sound of your commands, dear Christ, continues to ring in my ears: tell, bring health, raise, touch, kick out. May all the love I experience from you get acted out in my encounters with the people I meet today. Amen.

Don't Make a Scene

"When you enter a town or village, don't insist on staying in a luxury inn. Get a modest place with some modest people, and be content there until you leave. When you knock on a door, be courteous in your greeting. If they welcome you, be gentle in your conversation. If they don't welcome you, quietly withdraw. Don't make a scene. Shrug your shoulders and be on your way. You can be sure that on Judgment Day they'll be mighty sorry—but it's no concern of yours now."

MATTHEW 10:11-15

Ministry is not ingratiation. We must not conduct our lives of service so that people will like us; for if we do, we only become a servant to the neurotic needs of others, not a witness to the healthy promises of God.

How does it feel to have your witness rejected?

My commitment, Lord, is to you—not to success at any cost, not to acceptance by everyone. Keep me loyal, obeying your commands and doing your work, more interested in being faithful than in being popular. Amen.

Before the Son of Man Arrives

"Stay alert. This is hazardous work I'm assigning you. You're going to be like sheep running through a wolf pack, so don't call attention to yourselves. Be as cunning as a snake, inoffensive as a dove. Don't be naive. Some people will impugn your motives, others will smear your reputation—just because you believe in me. Don't be upset when they haul you before the civil authorities. Without knowing it, they've done you—and me—a favor, given you a platform for preaching the kingdom news! And don't worry about what you'll say or how you'll say it. The right words will be there; the Spirit of your Father will supply the words. When people realize it is the living God you are presenting and not some idol that makes them feel good, they are going to turn on you, even people in your own family. There is a great irony here: proclaiming so much love, experiencing so much hate! But don't quit. Don't cave in. It is all well worth it in the end. It is not success you are after in such times but survival. Be survivors! Before you've run out of options, the Son of Man will have arrived."

MATTHEW 10:16-23

We live, spiritually and morally, in hostile country. We need to be realistic about that. What we must not do is write doomsday endings to this experience. Family strife, social discord, church unrest are not the end. Christ is the end.

What hostility do you experience?

In each obstacle I meet today, Savior Christ, I will look for your help, anticipate your coming. Show me how to live in hard times with a light heart. Amen.

Be Pleased

"A student doesn't get a better desk than her teacher. A laborer doesn't make more money than his boss. Be content—pleased, even—when you, my students, my harvest hands, get the same treatment I get. If they call me, the Master, 'Dungface,' what can the workers expect?"

MATTHEW 10:24-25

We don't mind suffering for things we do that deserve punishment; but when we suffer for doing the right, we mind terribly. That is exactly what we let ourselves in for as Christ's disciples—misapprehension and rejection in pursuit of the good.

In what ways do people misunderstand you?

Lord Jesus Christ, I want to understand exactly the ways in which you expressed the truth, and I want to patiently submit myself to experiencing that way of life, not trying to get out of the hard parts, not complaining about the unpopularity, but enduring and remaining faithful. Amen.

More Than a Million Canaries

"Don't be intimidated. Eventually everything is going to be out in the open, and everyone will know how things really are. So don't hesitate to go public now. Don't be bluffed into silence by the threats of bullies. There's nothing they can do to your soul, your core being. Save your fear for God, who holds your entire life—body and soul—in his hands. What's the price of a pet canary? Some loose change, right? And God cares what happens to it even more than you do. He pays even greater attention to you, down to the last detail—even numbering the hairs on your head! So don't be intimidated by all this bully talk. You're worth more than a million canaries. Stand up for me against world opinion and I'll stand up for you before my Father in heaven."

MATTHEW 10:26-32

In Christ's kingdom no person is subordinated to a principle or a cause, used as a case history in a dissertation on goodness or sin. We are not treated as a means to anything; we are valued for who we are.

How many times in this passage are we encouraged not to be afraid?

When I look, Lord, at what other people do and say I become fearful—and rightly so, for my life to them is merely something to manipulate. But when I listen to what you say and believe in what you are doing, I trust, sure that revelation will triumph over hiddenness and resurrection over destruction. Amen.

You Don't Deserve Me

"If you turn tail and run, do you think I'll cover for you? Don't think I've come to make life cozy. I've come to cut—make a sharp knife-cut between son and father, daughter and mother, bride and mother-in-law—cut through these cozy domestic arrangements and free you for God. Well-meaning family members can be your worst enemies. If you prefer father or mother over me, you don't deserve me. If you prefer son or daughter over me, you don't deserve me. If you don't go all the way with me, through thick and thin, you don't deserve me. If your first concern is to look after yourself, you'll never find yourself. But if you forget about yourself and look to me, you'll find both yourself and me."

MATTHEW 10:33-39

We commonly avoid conflicts and encounters that require decisions between the good and the best, between the convenient and the excellent. We sink into a quagmire of domesticity, security, and self-gratification. The result is a conglomerate arrangement of habits and associations that we misname "community," sometimes even "church." But Christ has something far better.

What has Christ come to do?

Better your knife-cut, Lord, than the world's peace. I want the clarity of sharp decisions, not the amoral smog of confused compromises. Separate me from the half-gods of this world; free me for total response to you. Amen.

A Cool Cup of Water

"We are intimately linked in this harvest work. Anyone who accepts what you do, accepts me, the One who sent you. Anyone who accepts what I do accepts my Father, who sent me. Accepting a messenger of God is as good as being God's messenger. Accepting someone's help is as good as giving someone help. This is a large work I've called you into, but don't be overwhelmed by it. It's best to start small. Give a cool cup of water to someone who is thirsty, for instance. The smallest act of giving or receiving makes you a true apprentice. You won't lose out on a thing."

MATTHEW 10:40-42

Our acceptance of others and our service to others do not have to agonize over who is worthy, over what takes priority: Christ is present in everyone, everywhere. Our acts of trust and compassion, of witness and help, are anticipated by his, and fulfilled in his.

What are some of the small acts you can do in your life?

I dream, Father, of doing great acts of service in your name; meanwhile there are little opportunities for help all around us. Keep me faithful in the small tasks, discovering your presence in overlooked people and in obscure places. Amen.

Are We Still Waiting?

When Jesus finished placing this charge before his twelve disciples, he went on to teach and preach in their villages. John, meanwhile, had been locked up in prison. When he got wind of what Jesus was doing, he sent his own disciples to ask, "Are you the One we've been expecting, or are we still waiting?" Jesus told them, "Go back and tell John what's going on: 'The blind see, the lame walk, lepers are cleansed, the deaf hear, the dead are raised, the wretched of the earth learn that God is on their side.' Is this what you were expecting? Then count yourselves most blessed!"

MATTHEW 11:1-6

Jesus didn't get popular applause for what he did; he didn't overwhelmingly convince everyone of his truth. Even John, who prepared the way for Jesus' ministry, had his doubts. God in Christ doesn't come among us to meet our expectations, but to save us from our sins.

Why do you think John was in doubt about Jesus?

I have a lot of questions, Lord God, especially when things aren't going well in my life. I wonder if you are doing your job, if you have included me in your plans. And then, by faith, I get a larger vision, comprehend a deeper hope, and bless you for your mysterious and glorious work. Amen.

What Did You Expect?

When John's disciples left to report, Jesus started talking to the crowd about John. "What did you expect when you went out to see him in the wild? A weekend camper? Hardly. What then? A sheik in silk pajamas? Not in the wilderness, not by a long shot. What then? A prophet? That's right, a prophet! Probably the best prophet you'll ever hear. He is the prophet that Malachi announced when he wrote, 'I'm sending my prophet ahead of you, to make the road smooth for you.' Let me tell you what's going on here: No one in history surpasses John the Baptizer; but in the kingdom he prepared you for, the lowliest person is ahead of him."

MATTHEW 11:7-11

Are we tourists, sightseeing in religion with binoculars and camera? Do we reduce the man of God to a spectacle? But the gospel is not a spectator sport; it is not window-shopping. God's rule has already broken in. The participation of the least, not the fame of the great, is what is important.

Why was John important?

It is a lot easier for me, Lord Jesus, to be an onlooker than a participant. I get all the pleasures of diversion and excitement and none of the stress of risk and discipline. But that is not what you want from me, and I know it. Forgive me for looking on, and enable me to enter in, by faith. Amen.

Take It by Force

"For a long time now people have tried to force themselves into God's kingdom. But if you read the books of the Prophets and God's Law closely, you will see them culminate in John, teaming up with him in preparing the way for the Messiah of the kingdom. Looked at in this way, John is the 'Elijah' you've all been expecting to arrive and introduce the Messiah. Are you listening to me? Really listening?"

MATTHEW 11:12-15

Intense listening is what is required from us, not religious poll-taking, not theological opinion-sampling. The spiritual danger that we face is casualness, the indifference that treats the Word of God on the same level as the newspaper editorial. True faith is energetic and single-minded.

Why is John compared with Elijah?

Your warnings, O God, are frequent and insistent — and necessarily so, for I let things slide, permit junk distractions to divert me from responding to your love and pursuing your will with my whole heart and mind and strength. Develop ardor in me, and keep me centered on you. Amen.

This Generation

"How can I account for this generation? The people have been like spoiled children whining to their parents, 'We wanted to skip rope, and you were always too tired; we wanted to talk, but you were always too busy.' John came fasting and they called him crazy. I came feasting and they called me a lush, a friend of the riffraff. Opinion polls don't count for much, do they? The proof of the pudding is in the eating."

MATTHEW 11:16-19

Every generation wants God to dance to its tune. And every generation complains that God doesn't meet its expectations—like bored and whining children. But it is God who makes demands on us, not we on him. It is God who includes us in his plans, not we who include him in ours.

What was the difference between John and Jesus?

I pick up the consumer mentality, Lord, and shop for religion the way I shop for groceries—sorting through the shelves (the churches!) to find what suits my taste. Forgive me. Let me be still before you and respond to all that you are for me, in faith, in adoration. Amen.

Doom to You!

Next Jesus let fly on the cities where he had worked the hardest but whose people had responded the least, shrugging their shoulders and going their own way. "Doom to you, Chorazin! Doom, Bethsaida! If Tyre and Sidon had seen half of the powerful miracles you have seen, they would have been on their knees in a minute. At Judgment Day they'll get off easy compared to you. And Capernaum! With all your peacock strutting, you are going to end up in the abyss. If the people of Sodom had had your chances, the city would still be around. At Judgment Day they'll get off easy compared to you."

MATTHEW 11:20-24

We can always look around us and find people who are more wicked than we are and feel that we are not so bad after all. We get justification by comparison. But God does not grade on the curve. We are not judged in comparison with others, but by our response to God.

Why is Sodom famous?

Have mercy on me, Christ. I see myself in the mirror of your word and see so much that I have done that is wrong, and so much that I have not done that is essential. I don't want to just get by with the approval of my peers, but to become whole by your grace. Amen.

Spelled Out

Abruptly Jesus broke into prayer: "Thank you, Father, Lord of heaven and earth. You've concealed your ways from sophisticates and know-it-alls, but spelled them out clearly to ordinary people. Yes, Father, that's the way you like to work." Jesus resumed talking to the people, but now tenderly. "The Father has given me all things to do and say. This is a unique Father-Son operation, coming out of Father and Son intimacies and knowledge. No one knows the Son the way the Father does, nor the Father the way the Son does. But I'm not keeping it to myself; I'm ready to go over it line by line with anyone willing to listen."

MATTHEW 11:25-27

God shows himself; he does not hide himself. God delights in letting us in on his plans and actions; he does not tease us with coquettish hints. There is mystery in the gospel, true, but it is the mystery of light, not darkness, or more reality than we can take in, not arcane secrets withheld from us.

What is the most important truth revealed to you?

I am full of praise, Lord God, for all that you show me, for everything that you reveal to me. I thank you for including me in what you are doing so that I can participate intelligently, for telling me what you are doing so that I can live in the light and not stumble in the dark. Amen.

Come to Me

"Are you tired? Worn out? Burned out on religion? Come to me. Get away with me and you'll recover your life. I'll show you how to take a real rest. Walk with me and work with me—watch how I do it. Learn the unforced rhythms of grace. I won't lay anything heavy or ill-fitting on you. Keep company with me and you'll learn to live freely and lightly."

MATTHEW 11:28-30

The day teems with possibilities. Jesus' command rouses us out of a sleepy timidity. He doesn't tell us to go out into the world and conquer it; he calls us into a yoked companionship with himself. He doesn't ask us to do anything that he doesn't promise to do with us. We are not so much sent out as invited along.

What does keeping company with Jesus look like in your life?

"Come unto Me, ye weary, and I will give you rest. O Blessed voice of Jesus, which comes to hearts oppressed! It tells of benediction, of pardon, grace, and peace, of joy that hath no ending, of love which cannot cease."[18] *Amen.*

In Charge of the Sabbath

One Sabbath, Jesus was strolling with his disciples through a field of ripe grain. Hungry, the disciples were pulling off the heads of grain and munching on them. Some Pharisees reported them to Jesus: "Your disciples are breaking the Sabbath rules!" Jesus said, "Really? Didn't you ever read what David and his companions did when they were hungry, how they entered the sanctuary and ate fresh bread off the altar, bread that no one but priests were allowed to eat? And didn't you ever read in God's Law that priests carrying out their Temple duties break Sabbath rules all the time and it's not held against them? There is far more at stake here than religion. If you had any idea what this Scripture meant—'I prefer a flexible heart to an inflexible ritual'—you wouldn't be nitpicking like this. The Son of Man is no lackey to the Sabbath; he's in charge."

MATTHEW 12:1-8

Jesus concentrates on the personal. He cuts through the maze of regulations and customs that we accumulate and elaborate, and discovers the essential act, the core truth. Jesus is full of refreshing common sense.

Review 1 Samuel 21:1-6 as background.

Father, so many things—ideas, customs, concerns—intrude themselves into my life and separate me from devotion to you. Put all these things in their place so that I can be in my proper place, worshiping you and living in love in the world. Amen.

How to Ruin Him

When Jesus left the field, he entered their meeting place. There was a man there with a crippled hand. They said to Jesus, "Is it legal to heal on the Sabbath?" They were baiting him. He replied, "Is there a person here who, finding one of your lambs fallen into a ravine, wouldn't, even though it was a Sabbath, pull it out? Surely kindness to people is as legal as kindness to animals!" Then he said to the man, "Hold out your hand." He held it out and it was healed. The Pharisees walked out furious, sputtering about how they were going to ruin Jesus.

MATTHEW 12:9-14

Jonathan Swift once remarked, "Most of us have just enough religion to make us hate, but not enough to make us love." Here is an instance of it, people hating Jesus. The list of crimes planned and committed on behalf of the deity stretches into a long list.

Why were they plotting? Did they hate Jesus?

Like so many others, God, I want your stamp of approval on what I find comfortable, not a life of repentance and risky faith. Keep watch over my heart today. Quickly expose any scheming that masks itself as "religious concern" but has as its actual purpose the murderous removal of the Redeemer. Amen.

Some Devil Trick

Jesus, knowing they were out to get him, moved on. A lot of people followed him, and he healed them all. He also cautioned them to keep it quiet, following guidelines set down by Isaiah: "Look well at my handpicked servant; I love him so much, take such delight in him. I've placed my Spirit on him; he'll decree justice to the nations. But he won't yell, won't raise his voice; there'll be no commotion in the streets. He won't walk over anyone's feelings, won't push you into a corner. Before you know it, his justice will triumph; the mere sound of his name will signal hope, even among far-off unbelievers." Next a poor demon-afflicted wretch, both blind and deaf, was set down before him. Jesus healed him, gave him his sight and hearing. The people who saw it were impressed—"This has to be the Son of David!" But the Pharisees, when they heard the report, were cynical. "Black magic," they said. "Some devil trick he's pulled from his sleeve." Jesus confronted their slander. "A judge who gives opposite verdicts on the same person cancels himself out; a family that's in a constant squabble disintegrates; if Satan banishes Satan, is there any Satan left? If you're slinging devil mud at me, calling me a devil kicking out devils, doesn't the same mud stick to your exorcists? But if it's by *God's* power that I am sending the evil spirits packing, then God's kingdom is here for sure. How in the world do you think it's possible in broad daylight to enter the house of an awake, able-bodied man and walk off with his possessions unless you tie him up first? Tie him up, though, and you can clean him out. This is war, and there is no neutral ground. If you're not on my side, you're the enemy; if you're not helping, you're making things worse. There's nothing done or said that can't be forgiven. But if you deliberately persist in your slanders against God's Spirit, you are repudiating the very One who forgives. If you reject the Son of Man out of some misunderstanding, the Holy Spirit can forgive you, but when you reject the Holy Spirit, you're sawing off the branch on which you're sitting, severing by your own perversity all connection with the One who forgives."

MATTHEW 12:15-32

People are always ready with an explanation of reality that eliminates God from their lives—anything to avoid dealing with the love of Christ. Our world is full of debunking, cynical explanations that flatten people and events into a sidewalk sameness.

Why is Jesus so vehement in his response?

Almighty God, I don't want to be in that crowd of people who are standing around on the sidelines criticizing and quibbling; I want to be with those disciples who are listening, and believing, and following. Amen.

The Power of Words

"If you grow a healthy tree, you'll pick healthy fruit. If you grow a diseased tree, you'll pick worm-eaten fruit. The fruit tells you about the tree. You have minds like a snake pit! How do you suppose what you say is worth anything when you are so foul-minded? It's your heart, not the dictionary, that gives meaning to your words. A good person produces good deeds and words season after season. An evil person is a blight on the orchard. Let me tell you something: Every one of these careless words is going to come back to haunt you. There will be a time of Reckoning. Words are powerful; take them seriously. Words can be your salvation. Words can also be your damnation."

MATTHEW 12:33-37

"But I didn't really mean it." The excuse is familiar but unacceptable. Every word reveals what is already in the heart. Whatever the heart is full of, whether good or bad, spills out in the words of our mouths.

What do your words reveal about your heart?

Root, O God, my life deeply in your redeeming work so that the words that casually and accidentally come from my mouth will be words of praise and exclamations of trust. Amen.

Jonah-Evidence

Later a few religion scholars and Pharisees got on him. "Teacher, we want to see your credentials. Give us some hard evidence that God is in this. How about a miracle?" Jesus said, "You're looking for proof, but you're looking for the wrong kind. All you want is something to titillate your curiosity, satisfy your lust for miracles. The only proof you're going to get is what looks like the absence of proof: Jonah-evidence. Like Jonah, three days and nights in the fish's belly, the Son of Man will be gone three days and nights in a deep grave. On Judgment Day, the Ninevites will stand up and give evidence that will condemn this generation, because when Jonah preached to them they changed their lives. A far greater preacher than Jonah is here, and you squabble about 'proofs.' On Judgment Day, the Queen of Sheba will come forward and bring evidence that will condemn this generation, because she traveled from a far corner of the earth to listen to wise Solomon. Wisdom far greater than Solomon's is right in front of you, and you quibble over 'evidence.'"

MATTHEW 12:38-42

Evidence of God's presence and action is accumulating all around us in enormous quantities. If we don't see it, it is because we are looking for the wrong things — for marvels and for sensations instead of for grace and resurrection.

What evidence are you looking for?

Train my eyes, O God, to see what is to be seen in Christ — new life from the dead, fresh hope from the grave, divine love renewing human emptiness. Amen.

Far Worse

"When a defiling evil spirit is expelled from someone, it drifts along through the desert looking for an oasis, some unsuspecting soul it can bedevil. When it doesn't find anyone, it says, 'I'll go back to my old haunt.' On return it finds the person spotlessly clean, but vacant. It then runs out and rounds up seven other spirits more evil than itself and they all move in, whooping it up. That person ends up far worse off than if he'd never gotten cleaned up in the first place. That's what this generation is like: You may think you have cleaned out the junk from your lives and gotten ready for God, but you weren't hospitable to my kingdom message, and now all the devils are moving back in."

MATTHEW 12:43-45

The goal of the Christian way is not human purity, but divine fellowship. Our task is not to sweep and beautify the house so that there is not a speck of evil dust to be found, but to invite our Lord to dwell with us and fill the house with the laughter of forgiveness and the conversation of grace.

How do you apply this Scripture to your life?

Lord, you know how I am always coming up with a new scheme for self-improvement and reducing my role in the spiritual life to that of char-woman, scrubbing and dusting and polishing my moral image. What I need is you, your presence. Come into my heart, Lord Jesus! Amen.

My Mother and Brothers

While he was still talking to the crowd, his mother and brothers showed up. They were outside trying to get a message to him. Someone told Jesus, "Your mother and brothers are out here, wanting to speak with you." Jesus didn't respond directly, but said, "Who do you think my mother and brothers are?". He then stretched out his hand toward his disciples. "Look closely. These are my mother and brothers. Obedience is thicker than blood. The person who obeys my heavenly Father's will is my brother and sister and mother."

MATTHEW 12:46-50

No one is born into an intimate relationship with Christ. We cannot presume on him. But everyone has access to an intimate life with him — a life of mother or brother or sister. No one is left out by accident of birth; everyone is included by an act of faith.

What is your relationship with Christ?

Lord Jesus, thank you for the newfound intimacies of faith — that there is a family in which all are accepted equally, all loved uniquely, and that I am included in the "all." Amen.

Listen

At about that same time Jesus left the house and sat on the beach. In no time at all a crowd gathered along the shoreline, forcing him to get into a boat. Using the boat as a pulpit, he addressed his congregation, telling stories. "What do you make of this? A farmer planted seed. As he scattered the seed, some of it fell on the road, and birds ate it. Some fell in the gravel; it sprouted quickly but didn't put down roots, so when the sun came up it withered just as quickly. Some fell in the weeds; as it came up, it was strangled by the weeds. Some fell on good earth, and produced a harvest beyond his wildest dreams. Are you listening to this? Really listening?"

MATTHEW 13:1-9

Matthew, Mark, and Luke agree in making this the first of Jesus' stories. Every word God speaks to us is seed. We must not treat it casually, waste any of it in uncommitted enthusiasm, or permit it to be crowded into oblivion by the words of others.

What kind of earth are you?

Keep speaking, dear Christ, and keep me listening. Let your word take deep root in the soil of my life and bring forth a crop of faith and love and hope, a life lived to the praise of your glory. Amen.

Why Tell Stories?

The disciples came up and asked, "Why do you tell stories?" He replied, "You've been given insight into God's kingdom. You know how it works. Not everybody has this gift, this insight; it hasn't been given to them. Whenever someone has a ready heart for this, the insights and understandings flow freely. But if there is no readiness, any trace of receptivity soon disappears. That's why I tell stories: to create readiness, to nudge the people toward receptive insight. In their present state they can stare till doomsday and not see it, listen till they're blue in the face and not get it. I don't want Isaiah's forecast repeated all over again: 'Your ears are open but you don't hear a thing. Your eyes are awake but you don't see a thing. The people are blockheads! They stick their fingers in their ears so they won't have to listen; they screw their eyes shut so they won't have to look, so they won't have to deal with me face-to-face and let me heal them.' But you have God-blessed eyes—eyes that see! And God-blessed ears—ears that hear! A lot of people, prophets and humble believers among them, would have given anything to see what you are seeing, to hear what you are hearing, but never had the chance."

MATTHEW 13:10-17

The story is a tool for deciding, not discussing. For those who want to have conversations about God, the story is opaque. For those who will look and listen and pray, the story becomes a means for participation in the life of faith.

Why do you like stories?

Thank you, Lord God, for sharing your secrets with me, for speaking in love and listening in kindness. My life is filled with the sights and sounds of the gospel. How privileged I am! How blessed! Amen.

He Produces a Harvest

"Study this story of the farmer planting seed. When anyone hears news of the kingdom and doesn't take it in, it just remains on the surface, and so the Evil One comes along and plucks it right out of that person's heart. This is the seed the farmer scatters on the road. The seed cast in the gravel—this is the person who hears and instantly responds with enthusiasm. But there is no soil of character, and so when the emotions wear off and some difficulty arrives, there is nothing to show for it. The seed cast in the weeds is the person who hears the kingdom news, but weeds of worry and illusions about getting more and wanting everything under the sun strangle what was heard, and nothing comes of it. The seed cast on good earth is the person who hears and takes in the News, and then produces a harvest beyond his wildest dreams."

MATTHEW 13:18-23

Every aspect of life is given significance by the word that Christ addresses to us. We understand our empty, barren hours as a failure to respond to Christ, and we understand our full, fertile days as a result of Christ's triumphant word working in us.

What part of the story are you living today?

Father, interpret my life for me by means of these words so that I may understand everything that takes place today in relation to what you have done and are doing and will do. I don't want to evaluate anything in terms of my effort, but only in the light of your intention and love in Jesus Christ. Amen.

Thistles

He told another story. "God's kingdom is like a farmer who planted good seed in his field. That night, while his hired men were asleep, his enemy sowed thistles all through the wheat and slipped away before dawn. When the first green shoots appeared and the grain began to form, the thistles showed up, too. The farmhands came to the farmer and said, 'Master, that was clean seed you planted, wasn't it? Where did these thistles come from?' He answered, 'Some enemy did this.' The farmhands asked, 'Should we weed out the thistles?' He said, 'No, if you weed the thistles, you'll pull up the wheat, too. Let them grow together until harvest time. Then I'll instruct the harvesters to pull up the thistles and tie them in bundles for the fire, then gather the wheat and put it in the barn.'"

MATTHEW 13:24-30

Jesus shows no panic in the presence of evil. He does not give his seed-word greenhouse protection. He is confident that good seed has vastly better survival strength than thistles.

What thistles are in your life?

Dear Christ, train me in such trust that I am able to share your poise. No more doomsday gloom when I find a thistle in the garden! I want your confident, relaxed case in the face of the opposition. Amen.

Like a Pine Nut

Another story. "God's kingdom is like a pine nut that a farmer plants. It is quite small as seeds go, but in the course of years it grows into a huge pine tree, and eagles build nests in it." Another story. "God's kingdom is like yeast that a woman works into the dough for dozens of loaves of barley bread—and waits while the dough rises."

MATTHEW 13:31-33

Frequently, our excuse for being irresponsible is the claim that we are insignificant. Jesus' stories of mustard seed and leaven put a stop to that. It is the unnoticed, invisible movements of Christ in us that become the forests and banquets of his kingdom.

What insignificant, invisible obedience can you engage in today?

I keep looking, God, for the dramatic moment when I can engage in a glorious sacrifice for the faith; you keep presenting me with daily opportunities for belief and obedience and hope. Help me to forget my dreams of melodrama and accept the reality of your kingdom. Amen.

The End of the Age

Jesus dismissed the congregation and went into the house. His disciples came in and said, "Explain to us that story of the thistles in the field." So he explained. "The farmer who sows the pure seed is the Son of Man. The field is the world, the pure seeds are subjects of the kingdom, the thistles are subjects of the Devil, and the enemy who sows them is the Devil. The harvest is the end of the age, the curtain of history. The harvest hands are angels. The picture of thistles pulled up and burned is a scene from the final act. The Son of Man will send his angels, weed out the thistles from his kingdom, pitch them in the trash, and be done with them. They are going to complain to high heaven, but nobody is going to listen. At the same time, ripe, holy lives will mature and adorn the kingdom of their Father. Are you listening to this? Really listening?"

MATTHEW 13:36-43

We live in an antihistorical age. Everyone, it seems, has amnesia. We are immersed in "presentness." Both past and future are drained of content. Taught by Jesus, we comprehend the past as our own story and anticipate the future as his promise and live with sharp-edged gratitude and vivid hope.

What do you hope for?

Too many people around me, Lord, think of the future, when they think of it at all, with dread. Taught by you, I will anticipate it with joy, knowing that your will is done on earth as it is in heaven. Amen.

Everything

"God's kingdom is like a treasure hidden in a field for years and then accidentally found by a trespasser. The finder is ecstatic—what a find!—and proceeds to sell everything he owns to raise money and buy that field. Or, God's kingdom is like a jewel merchant on the hunt for excellent pearls. Finding one that is flawless, he immediately sells everything and buys it."

MATTHEW 13:44-46

The two stories have one word in common: "everything." There must be no equivocation, no hesitation, no calculation before God's offer of new life. All we have is traded in for all that God has for us.

What, for you, is included in the "everything"?

O God, I don't want to bring a bookkeeper's mind to the life of faith, anxiously adding up columns of what I must give, columns of what I might get. I give all and accept all. Amen.

Cull the Bad

"Or, God's kingdom is like a fishnet cast into the sea, catching all kinds of fish. When it is full, it is hauled onto the beach. The good fish are picked out and put in a tub; those unfit to eat are thrown away. That's how it will be when the curtain comes down on history. The angels will come and cull the bad fish and throw them in the garbage. There will be a lot of desperate complaining, but it won't do any good."

MATTHEW 13:47-50

Grading, judging, deciding on relative merits—all that is very much a part of the world's life. But we are not good at it—nobody is good at it. Leave it to the angels. The story emphasizes the reality of judgment, at the same time that it says we have no part in doing it.

Whom are you tempted to judge?

I know, Father, that you are the judge of all the earth and that you will execute your judgment both firmly and mercifully. I leave all that to you as I throw myself into the work of believing you and loving my neighbors. Amen.

Trained in God's Kingdom

Jesus asked, "Are you starting to get a handle on all this?" They answered, "Yes." He said, "Then you see how every student well-trained in God's kingdom is like the owner of a general store who can put his hands on anything you need, old or new, exactly as you need it." When Jesus finished telling these stories, he left there.

MATTHEW 13:51-53

The mixture of old and new is what Jesus does so well, and teaches us to do. The gospel does not specialize in either ancient history or modern problems, but rather develops the skills to appropriate diverse treasures of the kingdom for redemption goals.

How does God train you?

What a rich heritage of truth and experience you have given me, God. And what fresh and creative materials you hand me day by day in situations and people. Daily train me in the skills that will make me a good disciple. Amen.

Taken for Granted

[He] returned to his hometown, and gave a lecture in the meetinghouse. He made a real hit, impressing everyone. "We had no idea he was this good!" they said. "How did he get so wise, get such ability?" But in the next breath they were cutting him down: "We've known him since he was a kid; he's the carpenter's son. We know his mother, Mary. We know his brothers James and Joseph, Simon and Judas. All his sisters live here. Who does he think he is?" They got their noses all out of joint. But Jesus said, "A prophet is taken for granted in his hometown and his family." He didn't do many miracles there because of their hostile indifference.

MATTHEW 13:54-58

We do it too. We domesticate Jesus. We think we know all about him and precisely what he can do and cannot do. We label him and define him. Our sophomoric knowledge becomes a substitute for a faith in him.

Does familiarity with Jesus breed contempt?

Lord Jesus, don't let my minuscule knowledge of your humanity detract from the enormous mystery of your divinity. Keep me open in faith to the majesty and glory of your being, and responsive to your power to change and save. Amen.

Five Loaves and Two Fish

At about this time, Herod, the regional ruler, heard what was being said about Jesus. He said to his servants, "This has to be John the Baptizer come back from the dead. That's why he's able to work miracles!" Herod had arrested John, put him in chains, and sent him to prison to placate Herodias, his brother Philip's wife. John had provoked Herod by naming his relationship with Herodias "adultery." Herod wanted to kill him, but he was afraid because so many people revered John as a prophet of God. But at his birthday celebration, he got his chance. Herodias's daughter provided the entertainment, dancing for the guests. She swept Herod away. In his drunken enthusiasm, he promised her on oath anything she wanted. Already coached by her mother, she was ready: "Give me, served up on a platter, the head of John the Baptizer." That sobered the king up fast. Unwilling to lose face with his guests, he did it—ordered John's head cut off and presented to the girl on a platter. She in turn gave it to her mother. Later, John's disciples got the body, gave it a reverent burial, and reported to Jesus. When Jesus got the news, he slipped away by boat to an out-of-the-way place by himself. But unsuccessfully—someone saw him and the word got around. Soon a lot of people from the nearby villages walked around the lake to where he was. When he saw then coming, he was overcome with pity and healed their sick. Toward evening the disciples approached him. "We're out in the country and it's getting late. Dismiss the people so they can go to the villages and get some supper." But Jesus said, "There is no need to dismiss them. You give them supper." "All we have are five loaves of bread and two fish," they said. Jesus said, "Bring them here." Then he had the people sit on the grass. He took the five loaves and two fish, lifted his face to heaven in prayer, blessed, broke, and gave the bread to the disciples. The disciples then gave the food to the congregation. They all ate their fill. They gathered twelve baskets of leftovers. About five thousand were fed.

MATTHEW 14:1-21

A hillside of hungry families was changed into a well-fed congregation by Jesus' fourfold action: He took, he blessed, he broke, he gave. Those four acts continue to be reenacted, and our poverty transformed into affluence, wherever people gather in Christ's name.

How is this miracle continued into your life?

When I examine my own resources, O Christ, I never seem to have enough. When I worship you, I never seem to run out of blessing. Thank you for your abundance, for your never-diminishing power to meet my needs and complete my joy. Amen.

Courage

As soon as the meal was finished, he insisted that the disciples get in the boat and go on ahead to the other side while he dismissed the people. With the crowd dispersed, he climbed the mountain so he could be by himself and pray. He stayed there alone, late into the night. Meanwhile, the boat was far out to sea when the wind came up against them and they were battered by the waves. At about four o'clock in the morning, Jesus came toward them walking on the water. They were scared out of their wits. "A ghost!" they said, crying out in terror. But Jesus was quick to comfort them. "Courage, it's me. Don't be afraid."

MATTHEW 14:22-27

While the disciples had been struggling in the boat, Jesus had been praying on the mountain. Their work was getting them nowhere; Jesus, strong from his hours of prayer, gave them what they needed.

What is one of the most frightening times of your life?

Thank you for your prayers, Lord Jesus: for bringing God to me, for bringing love to me, for invading my terror with your courage, for saving me. Amen.

Master, Save Me!

Peter, suddenly bold, said, "Master, if it's really you, call me to come to you on the water." He said, "Come ahead." Jumping out of the boat, Peter walked on the water to Jesus. But when he looked down at the waves churning beneath his feet, he lost his nerve and started to sink. He cried, "Master, save me!" Jesus didn't hesitate. He reached down and grabbed his hand. Then he said, "Faint-heart, what got into you?" The two of them climbed into the boat, and the wind died down. The disciples in the boat, having watched the whole thing, worshiped Jesus, saying, "This is it! You are God's Son for sure!"

MATTHEW 14:28-33

Peter moved from brash, untutored enthusiasm, to disabling doubt, to reverent worship. We, like Peter, have to be rescued from the excesses of presumption and saved from the disabling doubt. Worship, not walking on water, is what we are created for.

In what ways are you like Peter?

So many times, God, I venture into things that are over my head, and instead of looking to you to command and direct I look at the impossible odds and the overwhelming difficulties and sink dangerously. "Master, save me!" Amen.

Touch the Edge of His Coat

On return, they beached the boat at Gennesaret. When the people got wind that he was back, they sent out word through the neighborhood and rounded up all the sick, who asked for permission to touch the edge of his coat. And whoever touched him was healed.

MATTHEW 14:34-36

The terrible loneliness of the ill is shown in their desire to touch Jesus. His willingness to be touched, to be intimate with people in need, shows that he shares his complete person, his body as his spirit, with those who crave contact with wholeness.

What do you need from God?

I reach out to you, Savior Christ, hardly knowing what I need much of the time, but knowing that I need you. And you are there, ready to change my emptiness into wholeness. Thank you for your love and compassion. Amen.

Blind Leading the Blind

After that, Pharisees and religion scholars came to Jesus all the way from Jerusalem, criticizing, "Why do your disciples play fast and loose with the rules?" But Jesus put it right back on them. "Why do you use your rules to play fast and loose with God's commands? God clearly says, 'Respect your father and mother,' and, 'Anyone denouncing father and mother should be killed.' But you weasel around that by saying, 'Whoever wants to, can say to father and mother, What I owed to you I've given to God.' That can hardly be called respecting a parent. You cancel God's command by your rules. Frauds! Isaiah's prophecy of you hit the bull's-eye: 'These people make a big show of saying the right thing, but their heart isn't in it. They act like they're worshiping me, but they don't mean it. They just use me as a cover for teaching whatever suits their fancy.'" He then called the crowd together and said, "Listen, and take this to heart. It's not what you swallow that pollutes your life, but what you vomit up." Later his disciples came and told him, "Did you know how upset the Pharisees were when they heard what you said?" Jesus shrugged it off. "Every tree that wasn't planted by my Father in heaven will be pulled up by its roots. Forget them. They are blind men leading blind men. When a blind man leads a blind man, they both end up in the ditch."

MATTHEW 15:1-14

Rules and traditions are useful. They are useful the way bark on a tree is useful: to protect the life within. They preserve truth, but they are not truth. All truth must be lived firsthand, from the inner life.

Why are rules dangerous?

O God, let me never suppose that because I have inherited a few rules and traditions, I therefore have the living truth. Keep me in touch with the immediate acts of faith that respond to your living word in Christ so that I am resilient and growing in grace, not stiff and fixed in old ways. Amen.

Put It in Plain Language

Peter said, "I don't get it. Put it in plain language." Jesus replied, "You, too? Are you being willfully stupid? Don't you know that anything that is swallowed works its way through the intestines and is finally defecated? But what comes out of the mouth gets its start in the heart. It's from the heart that we vomit up evil arguments, murders, adulteries, fornications, thefts, lies, and cussing. That's what pollutes. Eating or not eating certain foods, washing or not washing your hands—that's neither here nor there."

MATTHEW 15:15-20

We are always turning religion into something that we can control and use to demonstrate that we are all right: a system of rules, an arrangement of traditions. Jesus is always probing to the heart, showing us that our disposition, our faith, and our thoughts are at the center of our relationship with God.

What traditions do you have that are worthless?

Forgive me, merciful Christ, for trying to hide behind conventional morality when I should be opening up myself to you for deep and eternal healing. Examine my inner thoughts and create the kind of life in me that will live to the praise of your glory. Amen.

Mercy, Master!

From there Jesus took a trip to Tyre and Sidon. They had hardly arrived when a Canaanite woman came down from the hills and pleaded, "Mercy, Master, Son of David! My daughter is cruelly afflicted by an evil spirit." Jesus ignored her. The disciples came and complained, "Now she's bothering us. Would you please take care of her? She's driving us crazy." Jesus refused, telling them, "I've got my hands full dealing with the lost sheep of Israel." Then the woman came back to Jesus, went to her knees, and begged. "Master, help me." He said, "It's not right to take bread out of children's mouths and throw it to dogs." She was quick: "You're right, Master, but beggar dogs do get scraps from the master's table." Jesus gave in. "Oh, woman, your faith is something else. What you want is what you get!" Right then her daughter became well.

MATTHEW 15:21-28

The Canaanite woman with her bold simplicity, absolute lack of guile, and persistent directness teaches us how to ask Christ for what we need. Too often we elaborately and piously negotiate, rather than simply throwing ourselves on the mercy of our Lord.

How do you feel about the disciples in this story?

"Almighty God, who seest that we have no power of ourselves to help ourselves; keep us both outwardly in our bodies, and inwardly in our souls; that we may be defended from all adversities which may happen to the body, and from all evil thoughts which may assault and hurt the soul; through Jesus Christ our Lord. Amen."[19]

Four Thousand Ate Their Fill

But Jesus wasn't finished with them. He called his disciples and said, "I hurt for these people. For three days now they've been with me, and now they have nothing to eat. I can't send them away without a meal—they'd probably collapse on the road." His disciples said, "But where in this deserted place are you going to dig up enough food for a meal?" Jesus asked, "How much bread do you have?" "Seven loaves," they said, "plus a few fish." At that, Jesus directed the people to sit down. He took the seven loaves and the fish. After giving thanks, he divided it up and gave it to the people. Everyone ate. They had all they wanted. It took seven large baskets to collect the leftovers. Over four thousand people ate their fill at that meal. After Jesus sent them away, he climbed in the boat and crossed over to the Magadan hills.

MATTHEW 15:32-39

The meal is one of Jesus' favorite places for ministry. Here a quite ordinary picnic becomes, under Jesus' words and acts, a messianic banquet. The needs that food meets in our bodies, Christ meets in our lives.

Compare this with the earlier meal in Matthew 14:13-21.

Never permit me, Lord, to sit down to a meal without being at least dimly aware of your great precedent-setting actions, whereby inadequately provided food becomes, because you are present, abundantly experienced fullness. Amen.

Pharisee-Sadducee Yeast

Some Pharisees and Sadducees were on him again, pressing him to prove himself to them. He told them, "You have a saying that goes, 'Red sky at night, sailor's delight; red sky at morning, sailors take warning.' You find it easy enough to forecast the weather—why can't you read the signs of the times? An evil and wanton generation is always wanting signs and wonders. The only sign you'll get is the Jonah sign." Then he turned on his heel and walked away. On their way to the other side of the lake, the disciples discovered they had forgotten to bring along bread. In the meantime, Jesus said to them, "Keep a sharp eye out for Pharisee-Sadducee yeast." Thinking he was scolding them for forgetting bread, they discussed in whispers what to do. Jesus knew what they were doing and said, "Why all these worried whispers about forgetting the bread? Runt believers! Haven't you caught on yet? Don't you remember the five loaves of bread and the five thousand people, and how many baskets of fragments you picked up? Or the seven loaves that fed four thousand, and how many baskets of leftovers you collected? Haven't you realized yet that bread isn't the problem? The problem is yeast, Pharisee-Sadducee yeast." Then they got it: that he wasn't concerned about eating, but teaching—the Pharisee-Sadducee kind of teaching.

MATTHEW 16:1-12

The Pharisees wanted a Jesus who would dazzle and delight them with signs and miracles; Jesus was only interested in sharing the life of God that would change them into being people of faith who praise.

What are you interested in?

Will I ever, dear Jesus, get over the immature fantasies that dream of great signs and wonders? As if there were not enough of them provided already in both creation and salvation! Purge me from the leaven of sign-seeking so that I may live by faith and in adoration. Amen.

You're the Christ

When Jesus arrived in the villages of Caesarea Philippi, he asked his disciples, "What are people saying about who the Son of Man is?" They replied, "Some think he is John the Baptizer, some say Elijah, some Jeremiah or one of the other prophets." He pressed them, "And how about you? Who do you say that I am?" Simon Peter said, "You're the Christ, the Messiah, the Son of the living God." Jesus came back, "God bless you, Simon, son of Jonah! You didn't get that answer out of books or from teachers. My father in heaven, God himself, let you in on this secret of who I really am. And now I'm going to tell you who you are, *really* are. You are Peter, a rock. This is the rock on which I will put together my church, a church so expansive with energy that not even the gates of hell will be able to keep it out. And that's not all. You will have complete and free access to God's kingdom, keys to open any and every door: no more barriers between heaven and earth, earth and heaven. A yes on earth is yes in heaven. A no on earth is a no in heaven."

MATTHEW 16:13-19

At the same time that Peter realized and confessed that Jesus was the Christ, the one who reveals God to us, Jesus named Peter as the rock on which the church will be built. The moment that we make Christ our Lord, Christ makes us his foundation stones for the building of his living temple in the world.

Have you confessed that Jesus is your Lord and Savior?

Be Lord and Savior to me, dear Jesus. I receive your presence as God's presence; I believe your words as God's words to me; make me what you will, use me how you will. No longer my will but yours be done. Amen.

Anyone Who Intends to Come

Then Jesus made it clear to his disciples that it was now necessary for him to go to Jerusalem, submit to an ordeal of suffering at the hands of the religious leaders, be killed, and then on the third day be raised up alive. Peter took him in hand, protesting, "Impossible, Master! That can never be!" But Jesus didn't swerve. "Peter, get out of my way. Satan, get lost. You have no idea how God works." Then Jesus went to work on his disciples. "Anyone who intends to come with me has to let me lead. You're not in the driver's seat; *I* am. Don't run from suffering; embrace it. Follow me and I'll show you how. Self-help is no help at all. Self-sacrifice is the way, my way, to finding yourself, your true self. What kind of deal is it to get everything you want but lose yourself? What could you ever trade your soul for?"

MATTHEW 16:21-26

We want to follow Jesus, but like Peter we also want to tell Jesus where to go. Jesus doesn't need our advice; he needs our faithful obedience. Discipleship means learning how to listen to Christ, not getting him to listen to us.

What are the supreme conditions for discipleship?

"Jesus calls us: by Thy mercies, Saviour, may we hear Thy call, give our hearts to Thine obedience, serve and love Thee best of all."[20] Amen.

Changed Right Before Their Eyes

Six days later, three of them saw that glory. Jesus took Peter and the brothers, James and John, and led them up a high mountain. His appearance changed from the inside out, right before their eyes. Sunlight poured from his face. His clothes were filled with light. Then they realized that Moses and Elijah were also there in deep conversation with him. Peter broke in, "Master, this is a great moment! What would you think if I built three memorials here on the mountain—one for you, one for Moses, one for Elijah?" While he was going on like this, babbling, a light-radiant cloud enveloped them, and sounding from deep in the cloud a voice: "This is my Son, marked by my love, focus of my delight. Listen to him." When the disciples heard it, they fell flat on their faces, scared to death. But Jesus came over and touched them. "Don't be afraid." When they opened their eyes and looked around all they saw was Jesus, only Jesus.

MATTHEW 17:1-8

Because he makes himself so accessible to us, we are in constant danger of reducing Jesus to a hail-fellow-well-met. But there is a terrifying majesty in him that occasionally becomes apparent to us. When it does it is unthinkable that we should treat him as a cosmic buddy; we can only fall down in awe and worship.

What do you think of Peter's proposal?

Lord Jesus Christ, open my eyes to the reality of your glory, to the splendor of your loveliness. I worship you. I praise you. I center my life in you, and only you. Amen.

Don't Breathe a Word

Coming down the mountain, Jesus swore them to secrecy. "Don't breathe a word of what you've seen. After the Son of Man is raised from the dead, you are free to talk." The disciples, meanwhile, were asking questions. "Why do the religion scholars say that Elijah has to come first?" Jesus answered, "Elijah does come and get everything ready. I'm telling you, Elijah has already come but they didn't know him when they saw him. They treated him like dirt, the same way they are about to treat the Son of Man." That's when the disciples realized that all along he had been talking about John the Baptizer.

MATTHEW 17:9-13

Visions are not for telling. They are too easily turned into gossip — sensational stuff for entertaining dull lives. And they are not to be used for advertising in a world greedy for the latest novelty. Visions are for faith — to put a cosmic scaffolding around the passion.

How was John the Baptist like Elijah?

Thank you, O God, for showing me the essential identity of the Changed Christ and the Crucified Christ, the Christ who is one with me in suffering. Amen.

A Kernel of Faith

At the bottom of the mountain, they were met by a crowd of waiting people. As they approached, a man came out of the crowd and fell to his knees begging, "Master, have mercy on my son. He goes out of his mind and suffers terribly, falling into seizures. Frequently he is pitched into the fire, other times into the river. I brought him to your disciples, but they could do nothing for him." Jesus said, "What a generation! No sense of God! No focus to your lives! How many times do I have to go over these things? How much longer do I have to put up with this? Bring the boy here." He ordered the afflicting demon out—and it was out, gone. From that moment on the boy was well. When the disciples had Jesus off to themselves, they asked, "Why couldn't we throw it out?" "Because you're not yet taking *God* seriously," said Jesus. "The simple truth is that if you had a mere kernel of faith, a poppy seed, say, you would tell this mountain, 'Move!' and it would move. There is nothing you wouldn't be able to tackle."

MATTHEW 17:14-21

The world's program is self-improvement: resolutions and calisthenics. Jesus' program is faith and prayers: believing and praising. We fail in the work of grace and love when there is too much of us and not enough of God.

What do you find yourself unable to do?

What I usually do, God, when I find that I am inadequate for a task, is to find some way to become more adequate, and you seem to be telling me that what I need to do is to deepen my dependence on you. Amen.

Children Get Off Free

When they arrived at Capernaum, the tax men came to Peter and asked, "Does your teacher pay taxes?" Peter said, "Of course." But as soon as they were in the house, Jesus confronted him. "Simon, what do you think? When a king levies taxes, who pays—his children or his subjects?" He answered, "His subjects." Jesus said, "Then the children get off free, right? But so we don't upset them needlessly, go down to the lake, cast a hook, and pull in the first fish that bites. Open its mouth and you'll find a coin. Take it and give it to the tax men. It will be enough for both of us."

MATTHEW 17:24-27

The freedom of the Christian is not tied to economics or politics or a judicial system. It comes from a relationship between Father and son (and daughter). It is not achieved by human violence, but is the quiet result of divine grace.

Compare this with Galatians 5:1.

Instead of demanding the freedom that I don't have, show me how to discover and enjoy the freedom that I do have—the freedom that flows from being in relationship with you, Father, and which releases me to a life of service and praise. Amen.

Start Over Like Children

At about the same time, the disciples came to Jesus asking, "Who gets the highest rank in God's kingdom?" For an answer Jesus called over a child, whom he stood in the middle of the room, and said, "I'm telling you, once and for all, that unless you return to square one and start over like children, you're not even going to get a look at the kingdom, let alone get in. Whoever becomes simple and elemental again, like this child, will rank high in God's kingdom. What's more, when you receive the childlike on my account, it's the same as receiving me. But if you give them a hard time, bullying or taking advantage of their simple trust, you'll soon wish you hadn't. You'd be better off dropped in the middle of the lake with a millstone around your neck."

MATTHEW 18:1-6

Jesus is not asking us to do anything that he did not do himself. He entered our humanity in the form of infancy. All his commands and counsel were first lived out in his own life. As children before the Father, we live in expectant awe and joyous trust.

What is characteristic of children?

Return me, gracious Christ, to the basic realities of life that are conspicuous in children, but obscure and unattended in adulthood: an eagerness to believe, a readiness to receive, a willingness to love and be loved. Amen.

Chop It Off

"Doom to the world for giving these God-believing children a hard time! Hard times are inevitable, but you don't have to make it worse — and it's doomsday to you if you do. If your hand or your foot gets in the way of God, chop it off and throw it away. You're better off maimed or lame and alive than the proud owners of two hands and two feet, godless in a furnace of eternal fire. And if your eye distracts you from God, pull it out and throw it away. You're better off one-eyed and alive than exercising your twenty-twenty vision from inside the fire of hell."

MATTHEW 18:7-9

Jesus is ruthlessly intolerant of any word or act that delays or diverts us from entering into life with him. These are fierce words: only understandable when we realize that nothing less than everything — eternal life — is at stake.

What interferes with your life of faith?

Save me, Lord, from the world's lazy tolerance, which masks uncertain commitments and failed visions. Sharpen my instincts for survival so that I am alert to repudiate anything that would interfere with my relationship with you. Amen.

The One

"Watch that you don't treat a single one of these childlike believers arrogantly. You realize, don't you, that their personal angels are constantly in touch with my Father in heaven? Look at it this way. If someone has a hundred sheep and one of them wanders off, doesn't he leave the ninety-nine and go after the one?"

MATTHEW 18:10-13

God is not interested in percentages—even an overwhelming 99 percent is unsatisfactory to him. He wants everyone. He doesn't write off anybody. And that should keep us from ignoring or despising or forgetting anyone, even the least. Especially the least!

Who are the "childlike believers" in your life?

Forgive me, O God, for slighting people who are on the fringes of society and seeking out the people who are important and influential. Give me the shepherd's heart, always on the lookout for the lost and the hurt, after the manner of Jesus. Amen.

Two or Three

"If a fellow believer hurts you, go and tell him—work it out between the two of you. If he listens, you've made a friend. If he won't listen, take one or two others along so that the presence of witnesses will keep things honest, and try again. If he still won't listen, tell the church. If he won't listen to the church, you'll have to start over from scratch, confront him with the need for repentance, and offer again God's forgiving love. Take this most seriously: A yes on earth is yes in heaven; a no on earth is no in heaven. What you say to one another is eternal. I mean this. When two of you get together on anything at all on earth and make a prayer of it, my Father in heaven goes into action. And when two or three of you are together because of me, you can be sure that I'll be there."

MATTHEW 18:15-20

We would get on better if we could ignore or dismiss offending people. A private religion would be much more to our taste. But God will not permit it: We must learn God's forgiveness and love among people whom we forgive and love.

Who has hurt you?

Give me the courage, Lord Jesus, to face the people today who have displeased or hurt or troubled me. Help me to forgive them, not condemn them. By your grace draw me into a community with them where together we experience your presence. Amen.

How Many Times?

At that point Peter got up the nerve to ask, "Master, how many times do I forgive a brother or sister who hurts me? Seven?" Jesus replied, "Seven! Hardly. Try seventy times seven. The kingdom of God is like a king who decided to square accounts with his servants. As he got under way, one servant was brought before him who had run up a debt of a hundred thousand dollars. He couldn't pay up, so the king ordered the man, along with his wife, children, and goods, to be auctioned off at the slave market. The poor wretch threw himself at the king's feet and begged, 'Give me a chance and I'll pay it all back.' Touched by his plea, the king let him off, erasing the debt. The servant was no sooner out of the room when he came upon one of his fellow servants who owed him ten dollars. He seized him by the throat and demanded, 'Pay up. Now!' The poor wretch threw himself down and begged, 'Give me a chance and I'll pay it back.' But he wouldn't do it. He had him arrested and put in jail until the debt was paid. When the other servants saw this going on, they were outraged and brought out a detailed report to the king. The king summoned the man and said, 'You evil servant! I forgave your entire debt when you begged me for mercy. Shouldn't you be compelled to be merciful to your fellow servant who asked for mercy?' The king was furious and put the screws to the man until he paid back his entire debt. And that's exactly what my Father in heaven is going to do to each one of you who doesn't forgive unconditionally anyone who asks for mercy."

MATTHEW 18:21-35

Peter asked for a statistical count; Jesus gave him a story. We do not calculate forgiveness by numbers; we live it out in a world of incalculable mercy.

Whom do you need to forgive?

Your stories, Jesus, describe a world I can't really see, a world large with generosity. Every mean act and every failed task is released from condemnation. I want to share in this world, Lord, of forgiving and being forgiven. Amen.

Is It Legal?

One day the Pharisees were badgering him: "Is it legal for a man to divorce his wife for any reason?" He answered, "Haven't you read in your Bible that the Creator originally made man and woman for each other, male and female? And because of this, a man leaves father and mother and is firmly bonded to his wife, becoming one flesh—no longer two bodies but one. Because God created this organic union of the two sexes, no one should desecrate his art by cutting them apart." They shot back in rebuttal, "If that's so, why did Moses give instructions for divorce papers and divorce procedures?" Jesus said, "Moses provided for divorce as a concession to your hardheartedness, but it is not part of God's original plan. I'm holding you to the original plan, and holding you liable for adultery if you divorce your faithful wife and then marry someone else. I make an exception in cases where the spouse has committed adultery."

MATTHEW 19:3-9

Some people come to Jesus and say, "Help me; have mercy upon me." Jesus responds immediately and graciously. Others, like these Pharisees, come and say, "Is it legal . . . ?" They are interested not in what God can do for them, but in what they can get by with. All they get from Jesus is some quotations from Genesis.

What Scripture does Jesus quote?

Now, Father, I see why some of my prayers are unsatisfactory: I am interested in my possibilities rather than in your grace. I ask for information rather than for mercy. I see the difference; now help me to pray the difference. Amen.

Not Everyone Is Mature Enough

Jesus' disciples objected, "If those are the terms of marriage, we're stuck. Why get married?" But Jesus said, "Not everyone is mature enough to live a married life. It requires a certain aptitude and grace. Marriage isn't for everyone. Some, from birth seemingly, never give marriage a thought. Others never get asked—or accepted. And some decide not to get married for kingdom reasons. But it you're capable of growing into the largeness of marriage, do it."

MATTHEW 19:10-12

Jesus doesn't impose a uniform way of life on everyone. There are different ways of life in which to pursue a committed discipleship. God gives the means to accomplish the ends that he commands in us.

In what station in life has God placed you?

Create a contentment in me, God, with the circumstances of my life. It is so inwardly destructive to be always wishing I were in a different situation or involved in other relationships. Show me how to do the best in love and faith right where I am. Amen.

Lay Hands on Them and Pray

One day children were brought to Jesus in the hope that he would lay hands on them and pray over them. The disciples shooed them off. But Jesus intervened: "Let the children alone, don't prevent them from coming to me. God's kingdom is made up of people like these." After laying hands on them, he left.

MATTHEW 19:13-15

The extremities of existence are joined in Jesus' life: He touches children, immersing himself in the sensual, physical realities of the human; and he prays, laying hold of the unseen, spiritual realities of God.

Do you separate the physical and spiritual?

I want to be equally at home, Lord Jesus, in material, physical things and in spiritual, divine realities—in the same way that you were, touching and praying. Amen.

Give It All You've Got

Another day, a man stopped Jesus and asked, "Teacher, what good thing must I do to get eternal life?" Jesus said, "Why do you question me about what's good? *God* is the One who is good. If you want to enter the life of God, just do what he tells you." The man asked, "What in particular?" Jesus said, "Don't murder, don't commit adultery, don't steal, don't lie, honor your father and mother, and love your neighbor as you do yourself." The young man said, "I've done all that. What's left?" "If you want to give it all you've got," Jesus replied, "go sell your possessions; give everything to the poor. All your wealth will then be in heaven. Then come follow me." That was the last thing the young man expected to hear. And so, crestfallen, he walked away. He was holding on tight to a lot of things, and he couldn't bear to let go.

MATTHEW 19:16-22

The young man thought that he had kept the Levitical command, "Love your neighbor as you do yourself," but it had never occurred to him that his neighbor might be the poor man and that love had something to do with how he spent his money.

Who are some of the unseen "neighbors" in your life?

I know the commands, O God, but I need your help in seeing the people and circumstances where my obedience is commanded. Open my hands that have been clutching possessions; open my eyes too long blind to certain neighbors. Amen.

Any Chance at All?

As he watched him go, Jesus told his disciples, "Do you have any idea how difficult it is for the rich to enter God's kingdom? Let me tell you, it's easier to gallop a camel through a needle's eye than for the rich to enter God's kingdom." The disciples were staggered. "Then who has any chance at all?" Jesus looked hard at them and said, "No chance at all if you think you can pull it off yourself. Every chance in the world if you trust God to do it." Then Peter chimed in, "We left everything and followed you. What do we get out of it?" Jesus replied, "Yes, you have followed me. In the re-creation of the world, when the Son of Man will rule gloriously, you who have followed me will also rule, starting with the twelve tribes of Israel. And not only you, but anyone who sacrifices home, family, fields—whatever—because of me will get it all back a hundred times over, not to mention the considerable bonus of eternal life."

MATTHEW 19:23-29

We have to make a choice between possessing as much as we can manage, proving we are worth something by our visible wealth, and traveling light in faith, believing that we are worth everything simply because God loves us.

What have you left?

As long, Father, as I harbor covetous desires to be among the first, I am never free to respond quickly and spontaneously to your presence and your word. Forgive me for wanting to be among the rich, and for avoiding the company of the poor, where you are. Amen.

The Last First

"God's kingdom is like an estate manager who went out early in the morning to hire workers for his vineyard. They agreed on a wage of a dollar a day, and went to work. Later, about nine o'clock, the manager saw some other men hanging around the town square unemployed. He told them to go to work in his vineyard and he would pay them a fair wage. They went. He did the same thing at noon, and again at three o'clock. At five o'clock he went back and found still others hanging around. He said, 'Why are you standing around all day doing nothing?' They said, 'Because no one hired us.' He told them to go to work in his vineyard. When the day's work was over, the owner of the vineyard instructed his foreman, 'Call the workers in and pay them their wages. Start with the last hired and go on to the first.' Those hired at five o'clock came up and were each given a dollar. When those who were hired first saw that, they assumed they would get far more. But they got the same, each of them one dollar. Taking the dollar, they groused angrily to the manager, 'These last workers put in only one easy hour, and you just made them equal to us, who slaved all day under a scorching sun.' He replied to the one speaking for the rest, 'Friend, I haven't been unfair. We agreed on the wage of a dollar, didn't we? So take it and go. I decided to give to the one who came last the same as you. Can't I do what I want with my own money? Are you going to get stingy because I am generous?' Here it is again, the Great Reversal: many of the first ending up last, and the last first."

MATTHEW 20:1-16

Christ doesn't run the world by consulting us, asking what we think is right or proper. Naturally, we make our share of complaints against his administration. But much of our discontent, phrased as a concern for justice, is only petty envy and small-minded jealousy.

What don't you like about how God runs things?

You are right on target, Lord, when you ask me, "Do you begrudge my generosity?" It is not easy to get used to a life of extravagant mercy when I have grown up on nit-picking calculations of rights and benefits. Amen.

The Son of Man Will Be Betrayed

Jesus, now well on the way up to Jerusalem, took the Twelve off to the side of the road and said, "Listen to me carefully. We are on our way up to Jerusalem. When we get there, the Son of Man will be betrayed to the religious leaders and scholars. They will sentence him to death. They will then hand him over to the Romans for mockery and torture and crucifixion. On the third day he will be raised up alive."

MATTHEW 20:17-19

Association with Jesus puts us in the company of healing, enlightenment, and unanticipated joys. But it also puts us in the place of betrayal, humiliation, and crucifixion. We must, if we are faithful to the Christian way, accept the one as readily as the other.

Why is this announcement a surprise?

I will not forget, Lord Christ, when I experience apprehension and dread, that they are announced and documented parts of the life of discipleship. Keep me faithful in the difficult trials as you accompany me with the promise of resurrection. Amen.

In Exchange for the Many

It was about that time that the mother of the Zebedee brothers came with her two sons and knelt before Jesus with a request. "What do you want?" Jesus asked. She said, "Give your word that these two sons of mine will be awarded the highest places of honor in your kingdom, one at your right hand, one at your left hand." Jesus responded, "You have no idea what you're asking." And he said to James and John, "Are you capable of drinking the cup that I'm about to drink?" They said, "Sure, why not?" Jesus said, "Come to think of it, you *are* going to drink my cup. But as to awarding places of honor, that's not my business. My Father is taking care of that." When the ten others heard about this, they lost their tempers, thoroughly disgusted with the two brothers. So Jesus got them together to settle things down. He said, "You've observed how godless rulers throw their weight around, how quickly a little power goes to their heads. It's not going to be that way with you. Whoever wants to be great must become a servant. Whoever wants to be first among you must be your slave. That is what the Son of Man has done: He came to serve, not be served—and then to give away his life in exchange for the many who are held hostage."

MATTHEW 20:20-28

We attempt to get the respect and recognition of a life of discipleship by acquiring a few pious habits. Jesus demands a life that makes a difference: a life of service, a life of giving.

How do you live as a servant?

My confession, Lord: I keep hoping that being a Christian will give me an advantage over everybody else; I make a habit of looking for loopholes in your demands for a life of service. Forgive me, for Jesus' sake. Amen.

What Do You Want?

As they were leaving Jericho, a huge crowd followed. Suddenly they came upon two blind men sitting alongside the road. When they heard it was Jesus passing, they cried out, "Master, have mercy on us! Mercy, Son of David!" The crowd tried to hush them up, but they got all the louder, crying, "Master, have mercy on us! Mercy, Son of David!" Jesus stopped and called over, "What do you want from me?" They said, "Master, we want our eyes opened. We want to see!" Deeply moved, Jesus touched their eyes. They had their sight back that very instant, and joined the procession.

MATTHEW 20:29-34

The blind men's answer to Jesus' question seems obvious: "We want to see!" But had they ever asked for that before? Or had they long ago gotten accustomed to asking for handouts? Jesus challenges us to what is basic and essential: What do you really want?

What do you want?

Gracious Father, years of living in "Jericho" have turned me into a passive consumer, dependent on alms. My desires and wants are exceedingly trivial. You rouse in me soul-sized thirsts I had forgotten I had: I want sight. I want salvation. Amen.

Mount Olives

When they neared Jerusalem, having arrived at Bethphage on Mount Olives, Jesus sent two disciples with these instructions: "Go over to the village across from you. You'll find a donkey tethered there, her colt with her. Untie her and bring them to me. If anyone asks what you're doing, say, 'The Master needs them!' He will send them with you." This is the full story of what was sketched earlier by the prophet: "Tell Zion's daughter, 'Look, your king's on his way, poised and ready, mounted on a donkey, on a colt, foal of a pack animal.'"

MATTHEW 21:1-5

First-century Jewish expectation had fixed on Mount Olives as the site for the appearance of the Messiah. As Jesus prepared to present himself at the Jerusalem Passover, he partially fit into their expectations. At the same time, he confounded them by selecting a plodding beast of burden to ride rather than a dashing war horse.

Look at a map of the Holy Land and visualize the relation of Mount Olives to Jerusalem.

I want to be ready, Jesus, for your daily entrance into my life. I know that you will come to me. I also know that the way you will come will differ from my preconceptions. Prepare me to receive you as you will to come. Amen.

Exactly

The disciples went and did exactly what Jesus told them to do. They led the donkey and colt out, laid some of their clothes on them, and Jesus mounted.

MATTHEW 21:6-7

Simple obedience is a marvelous act: When we do what Jesus tells us to do, everything falls into place, things work out. Why do we think we have to improve on his commands, edit his instructions?

Are you basically an obeyer or a kibitzer?

Almighty and eternal God, speak your word to my heart, commanding what you will. And then work in me the grace of obedience enabling me in faith to carry out your word. Amen.

Branches from the Trees

Nearly all the people in the crowd threw their garments down on the road, giving him a royal welcome. Others cut branches from the trees and threw them down as a welcome mat.

MATTHEW 21:8

Festivity was in the air. Our custom at parades is to wave banners and pompoms; the Hebrews made a red carpet with garments and tree branches. They knew something celebrative was taking place in Jesus, and they wanted in on it.

What is celebrative for you in Jesus?

"Joyful, joyful, we adore Thee, God of glory, Lord of love; hearts unfold like flowers before Thee, opening to the sun above. Melt the clouds of sin and sadness, drive the dark of doubt away; giver of immortal gladness, fill us with the light of day."[21] Amen.

Hosanna in Highest Heaven!

Crowds went ahead and crowds followed, all of them calling out, "Hosanna to David's son!" "Blessed is he who comes in God's name!" "Hosanna in highest heaven!"

MATTHEW 21:9

Hosanna means "Save now!" It is a cry for help in the context of assured response. The Savior has arrived! Salvation is at hand! Everyone's life is at the point of change for the better. That which none of us can do for ourselves is done for us in Jesus.

Read Psalm 118:25-26 for the source of this cry.

"Thou didst accept their praises; accept the prayers we bring, who in all good delightest, Thou good and gracious King! All glory, laud, and honor to Thee, Redeemer, King, to whom the lips of children made sweet hosannas ring!"[22] Amen.

Shaken

As he made his entrance into Jerusalem, the whole city was shaken. Unnerved, people were asking, "What's going on here? Who is this?" The parade crowd answered, "This is the prophet Jesus, the one from Nazareth in Galilee."

MATTHEW 21:10-11

Many things are put together in this parade: the obedience of disciples, the generosity of the donkey's owner, the prophecy of Zechariah, the enthusiasm of crowds, the praise of God. The final week of Jesus' ministry opens with a celebration. It will conclude with a resurrection.

What part do you play in celebrating Christ's rule?

God, I want to find my proper place among people who praise you. By your grace every day is a festival of salvation. Put a palm branch in my hand and a song in my mouth as I join the people who know the joyful sound. Amen.

Hangout for Thieves

Jesus went straight to the Temple and threw out everyone who had set up shop, buying and selling. He kicked over the tables of loan sharks and the stalls of dove merchants. He quoted this text: "My house was designated a house of prayer; you have made it a hangout for thieves."

MATTHEW 21:12-13

Places of worship are bustling centers of activity: centers for discussion groups, work projects, social gatherings — and, of course, a brief prayer to get things started on the right note. Most churches could stand a good temple-cleaning.

Is prayer the central activity in your church?

When I next enter my church, Father, I will pray. I will not go to talk about you, or talk to my neighbors, but to address you and be addressed by you. Keep me faithful and attentive to the conversation that you are having with me in Jesus Christ. Amen.

From the Mouths of Children

Now there was room for the blind and crippled to get in. They came to Jesus and he healed them. When the religious leaders saw the outrageous things he was doing, and heard all the children running and shouting through the Temple, "Hosanna to David's Son!" they were up in arms and took him to task. "Do you hear what these children are saying?" Jesus said, "Yes, I hear them. And haven't you read in God's Word, 'From the mouths of children and babies I'll furnish a place of praise'?" Fed up, Jesus turned on his heel and left the city for Bethany, where he spent the night.

MATTHEW 21:14-17

The noise of the money changers never, apparently, had bothered them, but the noise of children was intolerable. How could they become so quickly accustomed to the clangor of commerce and be so short-tempered with the shouts of children? How can we?

What psalm does Jesus quote?

"Come, Thou Fount of every blessing, tune my heart to sing Thy grace; streams of mercy, never ceasing, call for songs of loudest praise. Teach me some melodious sonnet, sung by flaming tongues above; praise the mount! I'm fixed upon it, mount of God's unchanging love!"[23] *Amen.*

From Small to Large

Early the next morning Jesus was returning to the city. He was hungry. Seeing a long fig tree alongside the road, he approached it anticipating a breakfast of figs. When he got to the tree, there was nothing but fig leaves. He said, "No more figs from this tree — ever!" The fig tree withered on the spot, a dry stick. The disciples saw it happen. They rubbed their eyes, saying, "Did we really see this? A leafy tree one minute, a dry stick the next?" But Jesus was matter-of-fact: "Yes — and if you embrace this kingdom life and don't doubt God, you'll not only do minor feats like I did to the fig tree, but also triumph over huge obstacles. This mountain, for instance, you'll tell, 'Go jump in the lake,' and it will jump. Absolutely everything, ranging from small to large, as you make it a part of your believing prayer, gets included as you lay hold of God."

MATTHEW 21:18-22

Jesus trains us to seek the essentials from God, to direct our longings and aspirations to the center. Prayer to God must become as common in our lives as conversation with our friends.

Is prayer central in your life?

God and Father, I find your love in and around me; I realize your salvation working deeply through my existence. Centered in you and surrounded by you, make every word I speak a prayer, in the name of Jesus Christ. Amen.

Who Authorized You?

Then he was back in the Temple, teaching. The high priests and leaders of the people came up and demanded, "Show us your credentials. Who authorized you to teach here?" Jesus responded, "First let me ask you a question. You answer my question and I'll answer yours. About the baptism of John—who authorized it: heaven or humans?" They were on the spot and knew it. They pulled back into a huddle and whispered, "If we say 'heaven,' he'll ask us why we didn't believe him; if we say 'humans,' we're up against it with the people because they all hold John up as a prophet." They decided to concede that round to Jesus. "We don't know," they answered. Jesus said, "Then neither will I answer your question."

MATTHEW 21:23-27

The question was not an honest request for information, but a tactic for avoiding personal responsibility. They asked questions about Jesus' credentials so that they would not have to answer the question Jesus' life posed to their lives.

Do you ever ask questions to avoid giving answers?

I want my life, Lord, to be an answer to your love for me: my actions and my words, my thoughts and my dreams—all a response to the great reality of your presence in Jesus, that calls into question my selfishness and my pride. Amen.

Which of the Two?

"Tell me what you think of this story: A man had two sons. He went up to the first and said, 'Son, go out for the day and work in the vineyard.' The son answered, 'I don't want to.' Later on he thought better of it and went. The father gave the same command to the second son. He answered, 'Sure, glad to.' But he never went. Which of the two sons did what the father asked?" They said, "The first." Jesus said, "Yes, and I tell you that crooks and whores are going to precede you into God's kingdom. John came to you showing you the right road. You turned up your noses at him, but the crooks and whores believed him. Even when you saw their changed lives, you didn't care enough to change and believe him."

MATTHEW 21:28-32

Our life is formed at the deepest levels not by protest and promises, arguments and resolutions, but by faithful obedience. In the silent depths of the soul, the responses formed finally result — in spite of doubts and denials — in a life pleasing to God.

Which of the two sons are you?

God in Christ: You probe my heart and discover behind the words that I speak the life that I live. Purify and sanctify that inner life so that I may please you and glorify your name. Amen.

What Will He Do?

"Here's another story. Listen closely. There was once a man, a wealthy farmer, who planted a vineyard. He fenced it, dug a winepress, put up a watchtower, then turned it over to the farmhands and went off on a trip. When it was time to harvest the grapes, he sent his servants back to collect his profits. The farmhands grabbed the first servant and beat him up. The next one they murdered. They threw stones at the third but he got away. The owner tried again, sending more servants. They got the same treatment. The owner was at the end of his rope. He decided to send his son. 'Surely,' he thought, 'they will respect my son.' But when the farmhands saw the son arrive, they rubbed their hands in greed. 'This is the heir! Let's kill him and have it all for ourselves.' They grabbed him, threw him out, and killed him. Now, when the owner of the vineyard arrives home from his trip, what do you think he will do to the farmhands?" "He'll kill them—a rotten bunch, and good riddance," they answered. "Then he'll assign the vineyard to farmhands who will hand over the profits when it's time."

MATTHEW 21:33-41

Popular-opinion polls condition us to look for truth in the percentages: Whatever most people do or think is the most right. The story exposes the foolishness of statistics: No matter how many times the farmhands rejected the truth, the truth remained to judge them.

What majority actions today do you think are wrong?

How faithfully you approach me, Lord Jesus! How persistently you enter my life. Open my eyes to your presence and my heart to your grace so that I will always accept your coming. Amen.

The Stone

Jesus said, "Right — and you can read it for yourselves in your Bibles: 'The stone the masons threw out is now the cornerstone. This is God's work; we rub our eyes, we can hardly believe it!' This is the way it is with you. God's kingdom will be taken back from you and handed over to a people who will live out a kingdom life. Whoever stumbles on this Stone gets shattered; whoever the Stone falls on gets smashed." When the religious leaders heard this story, they knew it was aimed at them. They wanted to arrest Jesus and put him in jail, but, intimidated by public opinion, they held back. Most people held him to be a prophet of God.

MATTHEW 21:42-46

All the experts who can't fit God into their thinking, or their living, conclude that there is simply no place for him. But they start in the wrong places. We don't fit God into our lives; he fits us into his. When we begin with him, the "head of the corner," our lives are fit for eternity.

What psalm does Jesus quote?

Too many times, O Christ, I have rejected you because you didn't meet my specifications. Forgive me for my shortsighted arrogance. Forgive me for my small-minded selfishness. Build me into the life you are making. Amen.

Only a Few Make It

Jesus responded by telling still more stories. "God's kingdom," he said, "is like a king who threw a wedding banquet for his son. He sent out servants to call in all the invited guests. And they wouldn't come! He sent out another round of servants, instructing them to tell the guests, 'Look, everything is on the table, the prime rib is ready for carving. Come to the feast!' They only shrugged their shoulders and went off, one to weed his garden, another to work in his shop. The rest, with nothing better to do, beat up on the messengers and then killed them. The king was outraged and sent his soldiers to destroy those thugs and level their city. Then he told his servants, 'We have a wedding banquet all prepared but no guests. The ones I invited weren't up to it. Go out into the busiest intersections in town and invite anyone you find to the banquet.' The servants went out on the streets and rounded up everyone they laid eyes on, good and bad, regardless. And so the banquet was on—every place filled. When the king entered and looked over the scene, he spotted a man who wasn't properly dressed. He said to him, 'Friend, how dare you come in here looking like that!' The man was speechless. Then the king told his servants, 'Get him out of here—fast. Tie him up and ship him to hell. And make sure he doesn't get back in.' That's what I mean when I say, 'Many get invited; only a few make it.'"

MATTHEW 22:1-14

We are faced with a life-or-death summons. The responses that we make to God in Christ are the stuff of eternity. The story administers a shock of realization that jars us out of our drifting dilettantism.

What part of the story speaks to you?

Lord, preserve me from such deficiencies of will and love that will keep me from being counted among the blessed celebrants in your presence. I know that I am among the called; grant that I will also be among the chosen. Amen.

Who Does It Look Like?

That's when the Pharisees plotted a way to trap him into saying something damaging. They sent their disciples, with a few of Herod's followers mixed in, to ask, "Teacher, we know you have integrity, teach the way of God accurately, are indifferent to popular opinion, and don't pander to your students. So tell us honestly: Is it right to pay taxes to Caesar or not?" Jesus knew they were up to no good. He said, "Why are you playing these games with me? Why are you trying to trap me? Do you have a coin? Let me see it." They handed him a silver piece. "This engraving—who does it look like? And whose name is on it?" They said, "Caesar." "Then give Caesar what is his, and give God what is his." The Pharisees were speechless. They went off shaking their heads.

MATTHEW 22:15-22

The question was designed to drive a wedge between the secular and the sacred, between what we owe to God and what we owe to society. But Jesus calls us to live in a world without partitions, to the glory of God, responsible to our nation.

How does this help you live well as a citizen?

I want my life, O God, to be consciously and deliberately lived under your sovereign lordship; but I also want to live responsibly as a citizen, through Jesus Christ. Amen.

At the Resurrection

That same day, Sadducees approached him. This is the party that denies any possibility of resurrection. They asked, "Teacher, Moses said that if a man dies childless, his brother is obligated to marry his widow and get her with child. Here's a case where there were seven brothers. The first brother married and died, leaving no child, and his wife passed to his brother. The second brother also left her childless, then the third—and on and on, all seven. Eventually the wife died. Now here's our question: At the resurrection, whose wife is she? She was a wife to each of them." Jesus answered, "You're off base on two counts: You don't know your Bibles, and you don't know how God works. At the resurrection we're beyond marriage. As with the angels, all our ecstasies and intimacies then will be with God. And regarding your speculation on whether the dead are raised or not, don't you read your Bibles? The grammar is clear: God says, 'I am—not *was*—the God of Abraham, the God of Isaac, the God of Jacob.' The living God defines himself not as the God of dead men, but of the *living*." Hearing this exchange the crowd was much impressed.

MATTHEW 22:23-33

Jesus has little patience with people who love nothing better than a good "religious discussion." He is interested in bringing people new life, bringing them into relationship with a living God.

Why did the Sadducees ask the question?

No empty disputes today, Lord, but empty tombs. I don't want to waste any time in clever arguments, but immerse myself intelligently in the Scriptures and respond devoutly to the living God. Amen.

Posing a Question

When the Pharisees heard how he had bested the Sadducees, they gathered their forces for an assault. One of their religion scholars spoke for them, posing a question they hoped would show him up: "Teacher, which command in God's Law is the most important?" Jesus said, "'Love the Lord your God with all your passion and prayer and intelligence.' This is the most important, the first on any list. But there is a second to set alongside it: 'Love others as well as you love yourself.' These two commands are pegs; everything in God's Law and the Prophets hangs from them."

MATTHEW 22:34-40

Most religious questions are not asked in order to acquire information or wisdom, but are used as frivolous camouflages for indolence. As long as we are asking questions, we don't have to do anything. Jesus' answer put a stop to the questions; his answer confronts us with the basic question of our lives. Will we love, or not?

What Scripture does Jesus quote?

What will it be for me today, Lord? Asking questions or loving in obedience? I don't need to know more, but I do need to love more. Keep me faithful to your command. Amen.

JUNE 27

Whose Son?

As the Pharisees were regrouping, Jesus caught them off balance with his own test question: "What do you think about the Christ? Whose son is he?" They said, "David's son." Jesus replied, "Well, if the Christ is David's son, how do you explain that David, under inspiration, named Christ his 'Master'? 'God said to my Master, "Sit here at my right hand until I make your enemies your footstool."' Now if David calls him 'Master,' how can he at the same time be his son?" That stumped them, literalists that they were. Unwilling to risk losing face again in one of these public verbal exchanges, they quit asking questions for good.

MATTHEW 22:41-46

Jesus answered the question by asking a question. We do not come to Christ to get answers; we come to have our lives called into question, and we find how our lives become an answer to him.

What question does Christ address to you? What is your answer?

"I find, I walk, I love, but O the whole of love is but my answer, Lord to Thee! For Thou wert long beforehand with my soul; always Thou lovedst me."[24] Amen.

Spit-and-Polish Veneer

Now Jesus turned to address his disciples, along with the crowd that had gathered with them. "The religion scholars and Pharisees are competent teachers in God's Law. You won't go wrong in following their teachings on Moses. But be careful about following *them*. They talk a good line, but they don't live it. They don't take it into their hearts and live it out in their behavior. It's all spit-and-polish veneer. Instead of giving you God's Law as food and drink by which you can banquet on God, they package it in bundles of rules, loading you down like pack animals. They seem to take pleasure in watching you stagger under these loads, and wouldn't think of lifting a finger to help. Their lives are perpetual fashion shows, embroidered prayer shawls one day and flowery prayers the next. They love to sit at the head table at church dinners, basking in the most prominent positions, preening in the radiance of public flattery, receiving honorary degrees, and getting called 'Doctor' and 'Reverend.' Don't let people do that to *you*, put you on a pedestal like that. You all have a single Teacher, and you are all classmates. Don't set people up as experts over your life, letting them tell you what to do. Save that authority for God; let *him* tell you what to do. No one else should carry the title of 'Father'; you have only one Father, and he's in heaven. And don't let people maneuver you into taking charge of them. There is only one Life-Leader for you and them—Christ. Don't you want to stand out? Then step down. Be a servant. If you puff yourself up, you'll get the wind knocked out of you. But if you're content to simply be yourself, your life will count for plenty."

MATTHEW 23:1-12

Most people do not start out to be hypocrites. We begin sincerely enough, with good intentions. But as it becomes easier to talk about God than engaging in the arduous process of deepening and growing in faith, we take the easier road. Outside fluency and expertise covers up inner sloth and emptiness.

Are you the same inside as outside?

God, especially when people look to me as some kind of authority on religion, I find it easy to take on the role, meeting their expectations, but ignoring yours. But I want my life to be an on-the-knees response to you, not an on-the-pedestal lording over others. Amen.

Frauds!

"I've had it with you! You're hopeless, you religious scholars, you Pharisees! Frauds! Your lives are roadblocks to God's kingdom. . . . You're hopeless, you religion scholars and Pharisees! Frauds! You keep meticulous account books, tithing on every nickel and dime you get, but on the meat of God's Law, things like fairness and compassion and commitment—the absolute basics!—you carelessly take it or leave it. Careful bookkeeping is commendable, but the basics are required. Do you have any idea how silly you look, writing a life story that's wrong from start to finish, nitpicking over commas and semicolons? You're hopeless, you religion scholars and Pharisees! Frauds! You burnish the surface of your cups and bowls so they sparkle in the sun, while the insides are maggoty with your greed and gluttony."

MATTHEW 23:13,23-26

Jesus' anger, verbalized in these lines of indignant thunder, sounds more terrifying after each repetition. The effect is cumulative. The hammering denunciations break up the false front of glib performance and expose the inner emptiness of self-centered smugness.

How many reprimands are pronounced in this passage?

Lord Jesus Christ, I accept the designation "Pharisee" and put myself under your prophetic analysis. Expose every tendency in me to separate the inner life of faith and the outer life of reputation; convict me of every instance of saying more than I am living. "Put me together, one heart and mind; then, undivided, I'll worship in joyful fear" (Psalm 86:11). Amen.

How Often

"Jerusalem! Jerusalem! Murderer of prophets! Killer of the ones who brought you God's news! How often I've ached to embrace your children, the way a hen gathers her chicks under her wings, and you wouldn't let me. And now you're so desolate, nothing but a ghost town. What is there left to say? Only this: I'm out of here soon. The next time you see me you'll say, 'Oh, God has blessed him! He's come, bringing God's rule!'"

MATTHEW 23:37-39

The most religious city in history was the site of the worst religious persecution. The place where God showed himself most completely was the place where God was rejected most vehemently. And the very streets where men and women shouted their hate, Jesus expressed the pathos that would finally convert them to singing hallelujahs.

Who are some of the prophets who were killed and stoned?

Forgive me, O God, for the many times I have rejected your words of invitation, your servants of love. I have not been as loud and public in my rejections as many, but my silent and private unbelief has been, all the same, a refusal. Amen.

A Pile of Rubble

Jesus then left the Temple. As he walked away, his disciples pointed out how very impressive the Temple architecture was. Jesus said, "You're not impressed by all this sheer *size*, are you? The truth of the matter is that there's not a stone in that building that is not going to end up in a pile of rubble."

M ATTHEW 24:1-2

The destruction of the temple was spiritual urban renewal—getting rid of an inadequate physical structure so that a "God-made, not handmade" one could be constructed in its place (2 Corinthians 5:1).

What was the purpose of the temple?

God Almighty, I don't want to become so attached to what my ancestors built in obedience to you that I miss the firsthand opportunities of participating in the new things you are doing in my generation. Amen.

Tell Us When

Later as he was sitting on Mount Olives, his disciples approached and asked him, "Tell us, when are these things going to happen? What will be the sign of your coming, that the time's up?"

MATTHEW 24:3

The view from where they sat was impressive: Jerusalem panoramic before them, with the magnificent temple in the foreground. But it is not what religious people build that makes the kingdom, but how and when a gracious God comes.

Do you spend most of your time looking at religious sights, or listening to Jesus' words?

Lead me into asking the right questions, Lord God of truth, and train me in a careful listening to your answers. I don't want to stand around looking at the religious scenery; I want to be alert to the new word you are speaking to me in Jesus Christ. Amen.

Doomsday Deceivers

Jesus said, "Watch out for doomsday deceivers. Many leaders are going to show up with forged identities, claiming, 'I am Christ, the Messiah.' They will deceive a lot of people. When reports come in of wars and rumored wars, keep your head and don't panic. This is routine history; this is no sign of the end. Nation will fight nation and ruler fight ruler, over and over. Famines and earthquakes will occur in various places. This is nothing compared to what is coming."

MATTHEW 24:4-8

A lot of people have franchises these days on predicting the future; it is one of the blue chip businesses in religion. The only thing worse than the crassness of the sellers is the gullibility of the buyers. Jesus warned us well and in detail—there is no excuse for any of us being deceived by these people.

Who has tried to deceive you by pretending to know God's timetable?

It is hard not to be impressed by these people who speak so urgently and convincingly about the future, Jesus; they all claim a direct commission from you. But then I return to these words of warning and their deceit is exposed. I am again content to be obedient at your feet. Amen.

Thrown to the Wolves

"They are going to throw you to the wolves and kill you, everyone hating you because you carry my name. And then, going from bad to worse, it will be dog-eat-dog, everyone at each other's throat, everyone hating each other. In the confusion, lying preachers will come forward and deceive a lot of people. For many others, the overwhelming spread of evil will do them in—nothing left of their love but a mound of ashes. Staying with it—that's what God requires. Stay with it to the end. You won't be sorry, and you'll be saved. All during this time, the good news—the Message of the kingdom—will be preached all over the world, a witness staked out in every country. And then the end will come."

MATTHEW 24:9-14

If we do not experience betrayal at this moment, we must not therefore become complacent and surprised if and when it comes. Betrayal, which was the fate of Jesus, is also the fate of his followers. Being a Christian is not a surefire way to get ahead in the world.

Have you experienced any of the forms of betrayal mentioned by Jesus?

I don't want my identity as a Christian to be shaped by the culture around me, but by the words that you, Jesus, address to me. How carefully you warned me to keep my guard up against the influencing attitudes of others, whether seductive or hostile. Keep me daily mindful of the dangers. Amen.

If Left to Run Their Course . . .

"But be ready to run for it when you see the monster of desecration set up in the Temple sanctuary. The prophet Daniel described this. If you've read Daniel, you'll know what I'm talking about. If you're living in Judea at the time, run for the hills; if you're working in the yard, don't return to the house to get anything; if you're out in the field, don't go back and get your coat. Pregnant and nursing mothers will have it especially hard. Hope and pray this won't happen during the winter or on a Sabbath. This is going to be trouble on a scale beyond what the world has ever seen, or will see again. If these days of trouble were left to run their course, nobody would make it. But on account of God's chosen people, the trouble will be cut short."

MATTHEW 24:15-22

If history were left to run its course, everybody receiving their moral deserts, the consequences would be merciless and inexorable. But we are not left to our fate; history is interrupted by mercy.

What do you most abhor in current history?

Sovereign and holy Christ: I listen and look at and read the news of the world, and despair—such absurd carnage, such mindless evil. And then I listen and look at and read your salvation and take hope—such mercy, such grace! Amen.

Don't Fall for It

"If anyone tries to flag you down, calling out, 'Here's the Messiah!'or points, 'There he is!' don't fall for it. Fake Messiahs and lying preachers are going to pop up everywhere. Their impressive credentials and dazzling performances will pull the wool over the eyes of even those who ought to know better. But I've given you fair warning. So if they say, 'Run to the country and see him arrive!' or, 'Quick, get downtown, see him come!' don't give them the time of day. The Arrival of the Son of Man isn't something you go to see. He comes like swift lightning to you! Whenever you see crowds gathering, think of carrion vultures circling, moving in, hovering over a rotting carcass. You can be quite sure that it's not the living Son of Man pulling in those crowds."

MATTHEW 24:23-28

The moment we believe in Jesus Christ as Lord and Savior, we quit believing a lot of other things. We quit believing in self-promoting preachers who say they have the latest word from God; we quit believing in schemes by which we can help ourselves to a fortune; we quit believing the puffery that puts religious leaders on pedestals.

Who and what don't you believe in these days?

You have made things so simple for me, dear Jesus. I simply believe in you. I don't have to take seriously everyone who speaks seriously in a religious tone of voice. Thank you for the simplicity of your life, saving me from the complexities of false Christs and false prophets. Amen.

Pulling in God's Chosen

"Following those hard times, 'Sun will fade out, moon cloud over, stars fall out of the sky, cosmic powers tremble.' Then, the Arrival of the Son of Man! It will fill the skies—no one will miss it. Unready people all over the world, outsiders to the splendor and power, will raise a huge lament as they watch the Son of Man blazing out of heaven. At that same moment, he'll dispatch his angels with a trumpet-blast summons, pulling in God's chosen from the four winds, from pole to pole."

MATTHEW 24:29-31

The terrible dissolution and falling apart of society and cosmos is decisively countered by the coming of Christ that signals a comprehensive coming together. "Coming together" is the last word, not "falling apart."

What Old Testament Scripture is Jesus referring to?

Come, Lord Jesus! Come and save your people, come and save your elect, come and establish your kingdom. Keep me faithful in prayer for you're soon coming and aflame in hope. Amen.

Won't Wear Out

"Take a lesson from the fig tree. From the moment you notice its buds form, the merest hint of green, you know summer's just around the corner. So it is with you: When you see all these things, you'll know he's at the door. Don't take this lightly. I'm not just saying this for some future generation, but for all of you. This age continues until all these things take place. Sky and earth will wear out; my words won't wear out."

MATTHEW 24:32-35

The earth looks so solid, the skies look so immense — and words seem so fragile. But it is the words that will endure, that are full of energy, and that accomplish our redemption, for Christ speaks them.

Reflect on the prominence of "word" in the gospel.

"O God of Light, Your Word, a lamp unfailing, shines through the darkness of our earthly way, o'er fear and doubt, o'er black despair prevailing, guiding our steps to Thine eternal day."[25] *Amen.*

Be Vigilant

"But the exact day and hour? No one knows that, not even heaven's angels, not even the Son. Only the Father knows. The Arrival of the Son of Man will take place in times like Noah's. Before the great flood everyone was carrying on as usual, having a good time right up to the day Noah boarded the ark. They knew nothing—until the flood hit and swept everything away. The Son of Man's Arrival will be like that: Two men will be working in the field—one will be taken, one left behind; two women will be grinding at the mill—one will be taken, one left behind. So stay awake, alert. You have no idea what day your Master will show up. But you do know this: You know that if the homeowner had known what time of night the burglar would arrive, he would have been there with his dogs to prevent the break-in. Be vigilant just like that. You have no idea when the Son of Man is going to show up."

MATTHEW 24:36-44

Jesus warned against getting anxiously upset by announcements of the end. Now he warns against complacently missing the signs of his arrival. In prayer we must be alert, but not gullible.

Do you have a lively sense of expectancy?

I never, O God, want to live in complacent sloth, soggy in religious routine, smug in pious satisfaction. I want to be expectant and ready for the new thing that you are doing today, and again tomorrow. Amen.

Overseeing the Kitchen

"Who here qualifies for the job of overseeing the kitchen? A person the Master can depend on to feed the workers on time each day. Someone the Master can drop in on unannounced and always find him doing his job. A God-blessed man or woman, I tell you. It won't be long before the Master will put this person in charge of the whole operation. But if that person only looks out for himself, and the minute the Master is away does what he pleases—abusing the help and throwing drunken parties for his friends—the Master is going to show up when he least expects it and make hash of him. He'll end up in the dump with the hypocrites, out in the cold shivering, teeth chattering."

MATTHEW 24:45-51

The ignorance of all of us (including the angels!) regarding the schedule of the coming again of Christ sets us free to go about our work of love without forever nervously checking the clock or calendar.

Do the predictors ever distract you from your work?

My curiosity, Lord, sometimes consumes me: I want to know when. And you draw me back into the fullness of this now, in which I can live by faith, content to receive what you give at the right time, and be steady at my work. Amen.

Ten Virgins

"God's kingdom is like ten young virgins who took oil lamps and went out to greet the bridegroom. Five were silly and five were smart. The silly virgins took lamps, but no extra oil. The smart virgins took jars of oil to feed their lamps. The bridegroom didn't show up when they expected him, and they all fell asleep. In the middle of the night someone yelled out, 'He's here! The bridegroom's here! Go out and greet him!' The ten virgins got up and got their lamps ready. The silly virgins said to the smart ones, 'Our lamps are going out; lend us some of your oil.' They answered, 'There might not be enough to go around; go buy your own.' They did, but while they were out buying oil, the bridegroom arrived. When everyone who was there to greet him had gone into the wedding feast, the door was locked. Much later, the other virgins, the silly ones, showed up and knocked on the door, saying, 'Master, we're here. Let us in.' He answered, 'Do I know you? I don't think I know you.' So stay alert. You have no idea when he might arrive."

MATTHEW 25:1-13

The story asks, "What's smart?" rather than "What's right?" Our minds as well as our morals are to be put to proper use in expectation of Christ's coming. Silliness is as much to be avoided in kingdom matters as wickedness.

How do you watch?

Dear God, you have given me careful teaching that you are coming, but not when. Keep me ever alert so that I am ready for whatever you have for me to do, whenever you choose to command me. Amen.

Delegated Responsibilities

"It's also like a man going off on an extended trip. He called his servants together and delegated responsibilities. To one he gave five thousand dollars, to another two thousand, to a third one thousand, depending on their abilities. Then he left. Right off, the first servant went to work and doubled his master's investment. The second did the same. But the man with the single thousand dug a hole and carefully buried his master's money. After a long absence, the master of those three servants came back and settled up with them. The one given five thousand dollars showed him how he had doubled his investment. His master commended him: 'Good work! You did your job well. From now on be my partner.' The servant with the two thousand dollars showed how he also had doubled his master's investment. His master commended him: 'Good work! You did your job well. From now on be my partner.' The servant given one thousand said, 'Master, I know you have high standards and hate careless ways, that you demand the best and make no allowances for error. I was afraid I might disappoint you, so I found a good hiding place and secured your money. Here it is, safe and sound down to the last cent.' The master was furious. 'That's a terrible way to live! It's criminal to live cautiously like that! If you knew I was after the best, why did you do less than the least? The least you could have done would have been to invest the sum with the bankers, where at least I would have gotten a little interest. Take the thousand and give it to the one who risked the most. And get rid of this "play-it-safe" who won't go out on a limb. Throw him out into utter darkness.'"

MATTHEW 25:14-30

All of us have times when it appears that everyone else has more than we do. We covet the more that others have, instead of devoting ourselves to use what we do have. Jesus has no patience with us at such times; his story is a prod to live our lives, just as they are, to the glory of God.

Do you ever use your inadequacy as an excuse to do nothing?

Help me to accept my status, Lord, and be thankful for what you have given me. And help me to boldly participate in the exchanges of love that will make a profit for your kingdom. Amen.

Sheep and Goats

"When he finally arrives, blazing in beauty and all his angels with him, the Son of Man will take his place on his glorious throne. Then all the nations will be arranged before him and he will sort the people out, much as a shepherd sorts out sheep and goats, putting sheep to his right and goats to his left. Then the King will say to those on his right, 'Enter, you who are blessed by my Father! Take what's coming to you in this kingdom. It's been ready for you since the world's foundation. And here's why: "I was hungry and you fed me, I was thirsty and you gave me a drink, I was homeless and you gave me a room, I was shivering and you gave me clothes, I was sick and you stopped to visit, I was in prison and you came to me." Then those 'sheep' are going to say, 'Master, what are you talking about? When did we ever see you hungry and feed you, thirsty and give you a drink? And when did we ever see you sick or in prison and come to you?' Then the King will say, 'I'm telling the solemn truth: Whenever you did one of these things to someone overlooked or ignored, that was me—you did it to me.' Then he will turn to the 'goats,' the ones on his left, and say, 'Get out, worthless goats! You're good for nothing but the fires of hell. And why? Because—"I was hungry and you gave me no meal, I was thirsty and you gave me no drink, I was homeless and you gave me no bed, I was shivering and you gave me no clothes, sick and in prison, and you never visited." Then those 'goats' are going to say, 'Master, what are you talking about? When did we ever see you hungry or thirsty or homeless or shivering or sick or in prison and didn't help?' He will answer them, 'I'm telling the solemn truth: Whenever you failed to do one of these things to someone who was being overlooked or ignored, that was me—you failed to do it to me.' Then those 'goats' will be herded to their eternal doom, but the 'sheep' to their eternal reward."

MATTHEW 25:31-46

The great acts of judgment are not arbitrarily imposed from the outside, they develop out of the ordinary actions of everyday life. The final kingdom has all its seeds in the acts of love and compassion of each day.

Do you think you will be surprised at the last judgment?

Thank you for this story, Jesus; now I know that everything counts. I will never again suppose that what I do is insignificant. I will look for your presence in every person I meet and serve you through each one. Amen.

By Stealth

When Jesus finished saying these things, he told his disciples, "You know that Passover comes in two days. That's when the Son of Man will be betrayed and handed over for crucifixion." At that very moment, the party of high priests and religious leaders was meeting in the chambers of the Chief Priest name Caiaphas, conspiring to seize Jesus by stealth and kill him. They agreed that it should not be done during Passover Week. "We don't want a riot on our hands," they said.

MATTHEW 26:1-5

While Jesus prophesied his death, his enemies plotted it. The rapt listening of the disciples was in contrast to the stealthy conspiring of the high priests. The world is divided between those who hang on Jesus' every word and those who plot to eliminate him from their lives.

Why were the priests against Jesus?

Lord Jesus Christ, how grateful I am that you have entered the arena of suffering and hurt and evil. If all I had were words spoken from a quiet hillside, I would not have what I need most—your victory over the worst, your presence in time of need. Amen.

Very Expensive Perfume

When Jesus was at Bethany, a guest of Simon the Leper, a woman came up to him as he was eating dinner and anointed him with a bottle of very expensive perfume. When the disciples saw what was happening, they were furious. "That's criminal! This could have been sold for a lot and the money handed out to the poor." When Jesus realized what was going on, he intervened. "Why are you giving this woman a hard time? She has just done something wonderfully significant for me. You will have poor with you every day for the rest of your lives, but not me. When she poured this perfume on my body, what she really did was anoint me for burial. You can be sure that wherever in the whole world the Message is preached, what she has just done is going to be remembered and admired."

MATTHEW 26:6-13

Devout living is not tightfisted stinginess, but something flaming, with alabaster extravagance. We do not grow in faith by hoarding and saving, but by pouring out generous acts of sacrifice in love.

Are you generous?

Save me, Lord Jesus, from the niggardly spirit that calculates and resents. Release me for a life that pours itself out without counting the cost, even as you poured yourself out for me. Amen.

It Isn't Me, Is It?

That is when one of the Twelve, the one named Judas Iscariot, went to the cabal of high priests and said, "What will you give me if I hand him over to you?" They settled on thirty silver pieces. He began looking for just the right moment to hand him over. . . . After sunset, he and the Twelve were sitting around the table. During the meal, he said, "I have something hard but important to say to you: One of you is going to hand me over to the conspirators." They were stunned, and then began to ask, one after another, "It isn't me, is it, Master?" Jesus answered, "The one who hands me over is someone I eat with daily, one who passes me food at the table. In one sense the Son of Man is entering into a way of treachery well-marked by the Scriptures—no surprises here. In another sense that man who turns him in, turns traitor to the Son of Man—better never to have been born than do this!" Then Judas, already turned traitor, said, "It isn't me, is it, Rabbi?" Jesus said, "Don't play games with me, Judas."

MATTHEW 26:14-16,20-25

It is difficult to comprehend that this act of betrayal could be committed by a man associated personally with Jesus, surrounded by peers in a common meal and intimate conversation. But any of us is capable of it: "It isn't me, is it?" is an honest question to ask ourselves.

Why did Judas do it?

Forgive me, Father, for the times that I have suddenly left the way of faith and gone off to execute a plan that I thought would bring me some short-term benefit. Amen.

The Bread and the Cup

During the meal, Jesus took and blessed the bread, broke it, and gave it to his disciples: "Take, eat. This is my body." Taking the cup and thanking God, he gave it to them: "'Drink this, all of you. This is my blood, God's new covenant poured out for many people for the forgiveness of sins.' I'll not be drinking wine from this cup again until that new day when I'll drink with you in the kingdom of my Father."

MATTHEW 26:26-29

The common elements of the meal, through Jesus' words and prayer, became the signs of our eternal salvation. The deepest spiritual truths are represented in the everyday material of bread and wine.

What does the Lord's Supper mean to you?

I receive what you give to me, Lord Jesus Christ—your life and your salvation. As I receive it, I live in hope, anticipating the full life of the kingdom, even as I am participating in it now by your grace. Amen.

Sheep Will Be Scattered

They sang a hymn and went directly to Mount Olives. Then Jesus told them, "Before the night's over, you're going to fall to pieces because of what happens to me. There is a Scripture that says, 'I'll strike the shepherd; helter-skelter the sheep will be scattered.' But after I am raised up, I, your Shepherd, will go ahead of you, leading the way to Galilee." Peter broke in, "Even if everyone else falls to pieces on account of you, I won't." "Don't be so sure," Jesus said. "This very night, before the rooster crows up the dawn, you will deny me three times." Peter protested, "Even if I had to die with you, I would never deny you." All the others said the same thing.

MATTHEW 26:30-35

Stumbling was a way of life for Peter, as it is for us. Optimism in our capacity for faithfulness is not the basis of our salvation. Our trust is in the resurrection.

When was the last time you stumbled?

I am grateful, God, that your plans do not depend upon my loyalty, that your salvation is not contingent on my steadfastness. Your resurrection takes place anyway. All praise to you, O God. Amen.

Do It Your Way

Then Jesus went with them to a place called Gethsemane and told his disciples, "Stay here while I go over there and pray." . . . Going a little ahead, he fell on his face, praying, "My Father, if there is any way, get me out of this. But please, not what I want. You, what do *you* want?" When he came back to his disciples, he found them sound asleep. He said to Peter, "Can't you stick it out with me a single hour? Stay alert; be in prayer so you don't wander into temptation without even knowing you're in danger. There is a part of you that is eager, ready for anything in God. But there's another part that's as lazy as an old dog sleeping by the fire." He then left them a second time. Again he prayed, "My Father, if there is no other way than this, drinking this cup to the dregs, I'm ready. Do it your way." When he came back, he again found them asleep. They simply couldn't keep their eyes open. This time he let them sleep on, and went back a third time to pray, going over the same ground one last time. When he came back the next time, he said, "Are you going to sleep on and make a night of it? My time is up, the Son of Man is about to be handed over to the hands of sinners. Get up! Let's get going! My betrayer is here."

MATTHEW 26:36,39-46

Sleeping, we slip into a private world, unconscious of God's action. Praying, the opposite of sleeping, explores every detail in the drama of existence, draws us into participation in Christ's passion.

What are some contrasts between sleeping and praying?

Live in me, Holy Christ; create a new Adam, a new Eve, to live to your glory in this garden. Teach me the freedom that lives your will instead of asserting my own. For Jesus' sake. Amen.

Cut and Ran

The words were barely out of his mouth when Judas (the one from the Twelve) showed up, and with him a gang from the high priests and religious leaders brandishing swords and clubs. The betrayer had worked out a sign with them: "The one I kiss, that's the one—seize him." He went straight to Jesus, greeted him, "How are you, Rabbi?" and kissed him. Jesus said, "Friend, why this charade?" Then they came on him—grabbed him and roughed him up. One of those with Jesus pulled his sword and, taking a swing at the Chief Priest's servant, cut off his ear. Jesus said, "Put your sword back where it belongs. All who use swords are destroyed by swords. Don't you realize that I am able right now to call to my Father, and twelve companies—more, if I want them—of fighting angels would be here, battle-ready? But if I did that, how would the Scriptures come true that say this is the way it has to be?" Then Jesus addressed the mob: "What is this—coming out after me with swords and clubs as if I were a dangerous criminal? Day after day I have been sitting in the Temple teaching, and you never so much as lifted a hand against me. You've done it this way to confirm and fulfill the prophetic writings." Then all the disciples cut and ran.

MATTHEW 26:47-56

Rome and religion conspired against Jesus and seized him, but he feared no evil. He was so sure of God's "shepherd's crook" (Psalm 23:4) that he was confidently dismissive of all "swords and clubs."

Where are you in this crowd?

You lived, Jesus, not by sword but by Scripture. Yet I continue to use violence, even when I am attempting to do right things. Teach me to do it your way—your goals, yes, but also your methods. Amen.

Caiaphas . . . Peter

The gang that had seized Jesus led him before Caiaphas the Chief Priest, where the religion scholars and leaders had assembled. Peter followed at a safe distance until they got to the Chief Priest's courtyard. . . . The high priests, conspiring with the Jewish Council, tried to cook up charges against Jesus in order to sentence him to death. But even though many stepped up, making up one false accusation after another, nothing was believable. . . . Jesus kept silent. Then the Chief Priest said, "I command you by the authority of the living God to say if you are the Messiah, the Son of God." Jesus was curt: "You yourself said it. And that's not all. Soon you'll see it for yourself: 'The Son of Man seated at the right hand of the Mighty One, arriving on the clouds of heaven.'" At that, the Chief Priest lost his temper, ripping his robes, yelling, "He blasphemed! Why do we need witnesses to accuse him? You all heard him blaspheme! Are you going to stand for such blasphemy?" They all said, "Death! That seals his death sentence."

MATTHEW 26:57-60,63-66

Caiaphas and Peter are mentioned in successive sentences. The high priest and the chief apostle both centered their attention on Jesus. Earlier, Peter had said "You're the Christ" (Matthew 16:16). Here, Caiaphas says it. The content of the gospel stays the same—but how different it sounds on the lips of Caiaphas and of Peter.

Why was Jesus silent?

A striking scene, Lord! The torture and mocking intended to reduce you to insignificance only reveal your strength. Out of this suffering your love appears with immense dignity and beauty. Thank you. Amen.

The Word Was First

"The Word was first, the Word present to God, God present to the Word."

JOHN 1:1

John and Genesis both fix our roots in God-reality: Our origins are in the God who speaks (and is therefore intelligible to us) and whose speech (Word) makes the very stuff of our existence.

Compare John 1 with Genesis 1.

God of creation, let all my "firsts" be in you: every thought, every act, every desire, every purpose, every plan. I want to be rooted and grounded in you, and you only. Amen.

Created Through Him

"The Word was God, in readiness for God from day one. Everything was created through him; nothing—not one thing!—came into being without him."

JOHN 1:2-3

It is impossible to separate what we know of God from who God is, what God has said from his very being. Everything that is made is a clue leading to God, and God, of course, is the truth of everything.

How did creation take place?

Thank you, Lord, for this gloriously intricate, put-together, held-together universe. Everywhere I look I find evidence of what you have done. Everything I see gives me another reason to marvel and praise. Amen.

The Life Was Light

"What came into existence was Life, and the Life was Light to live by."

JOHN 1:4

Our ability to see anything and understand it is because of God. Even our questions about God are evidence of God. Our enlightened minds, which we may use to deny God, are a gift of the God who gives us life.

What are some characteristics of light?

Father of lights, in whom is no variableness, neither shadow of turning, I thank you that "every desirable and beneficial gift comes out of heaven" (James 1:17). Amen.

Life-Light/Darkness

"The Life-Light blazed out of the darkness; the darkness couldn't put it out."

JOHN 1:5

In a contest between light and dark, light always wins. Darkness never smothers light; light always dissipates darkness. Darkness has no initiative and no energy. It is helpless against the pulsating radiance of the light.

What are some characteristics of darkness?

"This is the day of light: let there be light today; O Dayspring, rise upon our night and chase its gloom away."[26] Amen.

The Way to the Life-Light

There once was a man, his name John, sent by God to point out the way to the Life-Light. He came to show everyone where to look, who to believe in. John was not himself the Light; he was there to show the way to the Light.

JOHN 1:6-8

The contrast is abrupt: Our minds are drawn from the wide, cosmic sweep of creation to the rough Judean wilderness, where a man was calling particular attention to God's work and word in Jesus Christ.

What do you know about John?

By your word, God, the heavens were created, and by that same word, I am addressed. What is going on in the heavens and in my home are equally your interest. Make the connection in my faith between your grand purposes and your specific involvement in my life. Amen.

The World Didn't Notice Him

"The Life-Light was the real thing: Every person entering Life he brings into Light. He was in the world, the world was there through him, and yet the world didn't even notice. He came to his own people, but they didn't want him."

JOHN 1:9-11

That which is obvious in revelation and faith is not obvious to mere cleverness or doubt. "Think of it! The Word was made flesh and not one of the journalists of those days even knew it was happening!"[27]

Why was Jesus not recognized and not received?

Dear Lord, help me not to overlook the obvious—through carelessness miss the great signs of your saving love, through sloth have my eyes closed to the flashing lights of eternity, in Jesus Christ. Amen.

God-Begotten

"But whoever did want him, who believed he was who he claimed and would do what he said, he made to be their true selves, their child-of-God selves. These are the God-begotten, not blood-begotten, not flesh-begotten, not sex-begotten."

JOHN 1:12-13

New birth is a theme that recurs throughout John's gospel. All that we know of birth, naturally, is a kind of story of what God wills for us supernaturally.

Compare this with John 3:1-15.

Create, shape, and bring to maturity, Mighty God, the new life that you will for me in Jesus Christ. I want to be known as your child, be recognized as your child, and grow up into eternity as your child. Amen.

The Word Became Flesh

"The Word became flesh and blood, and moved into the neighborhood. We saw the glory with our own eyes, the one-of-a-kind glory, like Father, like Son, generous inside and out, true from start to finish."

JOHN 1:14

The "Word" by which God made all things (see verses 1-3) became an actual flesh-and-blood person, Jesus of Nazareth. A most astounding event, scarcely imaginable, but impressively documented in our gospels by those who saw it take place ("we saw the glory").

Compare this with Galatians 4:4-5.

Father, open my eyes to see all that you reveal in Jesus Christ. I don't want to miss a single instance of grace, nor overlook one item of truth. I want to see it all, your glory in Jesus. Amen.

This Is the One!

John pointed him out and called, "This is the One! The One I told you was coming after me but in fact was ahead of me. He has always been ahead of me, has always had the first word."

JOHN 1:15

John knew what to look for and what to expect—he was the first century's leading expert on the subject of Messiah. His years of preparatory preaching climaxed in his identification of Jesus as the Messiah sent and anointed by God.

How did John know that Jesus was the Messiah?

I thank you, dear God, for those teachers and preachers you have sent into my life to train me in what to look for and alert me to your living presence in Jesus Christ. Amen.

Gift After Gift

"We all live off his generous bounty, gift after gift after gift. We got the basics from Moses, and then this exuberant giving and receiving, this endless knowing and understanding—all this came through Jesus, the Messiah."

JOHN 1:16-17

God does not carefully calculate his stores of grace and truth and then cautiously dole them out in bits and pieces. He is lavish and extravagant as he reveals and shares himself in Jesus Christ.

How has God been generous to you?

God, what a change from what I was used to, living hand to mouth on morsels of law! Every day now is a banquet, grand and abundant! Thank you for this new lifestyle of "gift after gift after gift." Amen.

Plain as Day

"No one has ever seen God, not so much as a glimpse. This one-of-a-kind God-Expression, who exists at the very heart of the Father, has made him plain as day."

JOHN 1:18

In the words of Jesus, we know precisely what God says. In the actions of Jesus, we know accurately what God does. Jesus has taken all the guesswork out of thinking about and responding to God.

What does God look like?

God Almighty, whose ways are past finding out, thank you for your plain speech in a language I can understand, and your forthright actions in forms to which I can respond, in Jesus. Amen.

Thunder in the Desert

When Jews from Jerusalem sent a group of priests and officials to ask John who he was, he was completely honest. He didn't evade the question. He told the plain truth: "I am not the Messiah." They pressed him, "Who, then? Elijah?" "I am not." "The Prophet?" "No." Exasperated, they said, "Who, then? We need an answer for those who sent us. Tell us something—anything!—about yourself." "I'm thunder in the desert: 'Make the road straight for God!' I'm doing what the prophet Isaiah preached."

JOHN 1:19-23

John attracted much attention and was prominent in the public eye. He could have used the attention and popularity to build himself a following. It didn't even occur to him: He had only one aim—to announce Jesus as the Christ.

What Isaiah passage does John cite?

When people pay attention to me, Lord, I am apt to be flattered, pleased, and self-satisfied. Give me, instead, the grace to quickly refer all such interest to your love and grace and will in Jesus Christ. Amen.

Why Do You Baptize?

Those sent to question him were from the Pharisee party. Now they had a question of their own: "If you're neither the Messiah, nor Elijah, nor the Prophet, why do you baptize?" John answered, "I only baptize using water. A person you don't recognize has taken his stand in your midst. He comes after me, but he is not in second place to me. I'm not even worthy to hold his coat for him." These conversations took place in Bethany on the other side of the Jordan, where John was baptizing at the time.

JOHN 1:24-28

John's baptizing ministry fixed attention on our deepest need (sin) and God's greatest promise (forgiveness). But even while he did it, he made it clear that baptism was only sign-language—soon they would see and hear the actual words and authentic actions to which his ministry was mere prelude.

Why the reference to Elijah in the questions?

Don't let me ever, Lord Jesus Christ, get so interested in what others do in your name that I miss seeing your very presence; never let me get so caught up in questions and answers that I fail to hear you speak to me personally. Amen.

God's Passover Lamb

The very next day John saw Jesus coming toward him and yelled out, "Here he is, God's Passover Lamb! He forgives the sins of the world! This is the man I've been talking about, 'the One who comes after me but is really ahead of me.' I knew nothing about who he was—only this: that my task has been to get Israel ready to recognize him as the God-Revealer. That is why I came here baptizing with water, giving you a good bath and scrubbing sins from your life so you can get a fresh start with God."

JOHN 1:29-31

The lamb was the animal most connected in Israel's mind with forgiveness. Its use in sacrificial worship demonstrated that God had a way of dealing with sin and guilt. When John identified Jesus as God's Lamb, it meant that the great drama of forgiveness was about to take place before their eyes in him.

Compare this with Isaiah 53:7.

"When to the cross I turn my eyes, and rest on Calvary, O Lamb of God, my Sacrifice, I must remember Thee; remember Thee, and all Thy pains, and all Thy love to me: yea, while a breath, a pulse remains will I remember Thee."[28] Amen.

Like a Dove

John clinched his witness with this: "I watched the Spirit, like a dove flying down out of the sky, making himself at home in him. I repeat, I know nothing about him except this: The One who authorized me to baptize with water told me, 'The One on whom you see the Spirit come down and stay, this One will baptize with the Holy Spirit.' That's exactly what I saw happen, and I'm telling you, there's no question about it: *This* is the Son of God."

John 1:32-34

The descent of the dove was a sign that the Spirit of God dwelt in Jesus — the very life of God the Father was also the very life of God the Son. John's witness of the sign authenticated Jesus' identity as Messiah.

What are the characteristics of a dove?

"Spirit of God, descend upon my heart; wean it from earth; through all its pulses move; stoop to my weakness, mighty as Thou art, and make me love Thee as I ought to love."[29] Amen.

Two Disciples

The next day John was back at his post with two disciples, who were watching. He looked up, saw Jesus walking nearby, and said, "Here he is, God's Passover Lamb." The two disciples heard him and went after Jesus. Jesus looked over his shoulder and said to them, "What are you after?" They said, "Rabbi" (which means "Teacher"), "where are you staying?" He replied, "Come along and see for yourself." They came, saw where he was living, and ended up staying with him for the day. It was late afternoon when this happened.

JOHN 1:35-39

The test of John's integrity came when the time arrived to turn his disciples over to Jesus. He passed the test: He knew he had finished his preparatory work and so without reluctance turned those he had trained in repentance to follow Jesus in faith.

What is a disciple?

Help me, Lord Jesus, to be a good witness: quick to recognize your appearance, skilled at directing attention to you, and unhesitating in releasing people in my care to your care. Amen.

He First Found His Brother

Andrew, Simon Peter's brother, was one of the two who heard John's witness and followed Jesus. The first thing he did after finding where Jesus lived was find his own brother, Simon, telling him, "We've found the Messiah" (that is, "Christ"). He immediately led him to Jesus. Jesus took one look up and said, "You're John's son, Simon? From now on your name is Cephas" (or Peter, which means "Rock").

JOHN 1:40-42

The first impulse of those who are attracted to Jesus is generosity — not to get all we can, exclusively, for ourselves, but to share all we can with others. Andrew's generosity was evangelism.

Whom have you brought to Jesus?

I want to be a good witness to you, Lord God, so that none among family or friends or neighbors lacks an invitation into your presence because of rudeness or forgetfulness or selfishness on my part. Amen.

Nathanael

The next day Jesus decided to go to Galilee. When he got there, he ran across Philip and said, "Come, follow me." (Philip's hometown was Bethsaida, the same as Andrew and Peter.) Philip went and found Nathanael and told him, "We've found the One Moses wrote of in the Law, the One preached by the prophets. It's *Jesus*, Joseph's son, the one from Nazareth!" Nathanael said, "Nazareth? You've got to be kidding." But Philip said, "Come, see for yourself." When Jesus saw him coming he said, "There's a real Israelite, not a false bone in his body." Nathanael said, "Where did you get that idea? You don't know me." Jesus answered, "One day, long before Philip called you here, I saw you under the fig tree." Nathanael exclaimed, "Rabbi! You are the Son of God, the King of Israel!" Jesus said, "You've become a believer simply because I say I saw you one day sitting under the fig tree? You haven't seen anything yet! Before this is over you're going to see heaven open and God's angels descending to the Son of Man and ascending again."

JOHN 1:43-51

Nathanael was an open book to Jesus — as are we all. His surprise at Jesus' comprehensive knowledge of his background and character led him to an immediate confession of faith.

What kind of person was Nathanael?

God, your spirit searches the depths in me: discovers sin, whets an appetite for righteousness, prompts obedience, kindles faith. Search me deeply; know me thoroughly, in Jesus. Amen.

A Wedding in Cana

Three days later there was a wedding in the village of Cana in Galilee. Jesus' mother was there. Jesus and his disciples were guests also. When they started running low on wine at the wedding banquet, Jesus' mother told him, "They're just about out of wine." Jesus said, "Is that any of our business, Mother—yours or mine? This isn't my time. Don't push me." She went ahead anyway, telling the servants, "Whatever he tells you, do it." Six stoneware water pots were there, used by the Jews for ritual washings. Each held twenty to thirty gallons. Jesus ordered the servants, "Fill the pots with water." And they filled them to the brim. "Now fill your pitchers and take them to the host," Jesus said, and they did. When the host tasted the water that had become wine (he didn't know what had just happened but the servants, of course, knew), he called out to the bridegroom, "Everybody I know begins with their finest wines and after the guests have had their fill brings in the cheap stuff. But you've saved the best till now!"

JOHN 2:1-10

As the first sign of Jesus' ministry, the miracle at Cana establishes joy at the center of all that Jesus does. Exuberance surrounds all our Lord's words and work. Salvation is life plus.

What was the result of the sign at Cana?

You do this a lot, Lord: Just when I think there is nothing that can be done, with life reduced to mere survival and all resources exhausted, you step in and miraculously restore the joy, better than anything I thought possible. Thank you. Amen.

Capernaum

After this he went down to Capernaum along with his mother, brothers, and disciples, and stayed several days.

JOHN 2:12

Jesus' work was not always in public, out where people could see it. There were also quiet interludes of retirement and rest. The quiet asides are as characteristic of his ministry as the glorious signs.

Where is Capernaum?

In this moment of quiet prayer, Father, so center my heart in your will and grace that all my actions and words today may flow from you as a cool stream from its subterranean source. Amen.

Zeal for Your House

When the Passover Feast, celebrated each spring by the Jews, was about to take place, Jesus traveled up to Jerusalem. He found the Temple teeming with people selling cattle and sheep and doves. The loan sharks were also there in full strength. Jesus put together a whip out of strips of leather and chased them out of the Temple, stampeding the sheep and cattle, upending the tables of the loan sharks, spilling coins left and right. He told the dove merchants, "Get your things out of here! Stop turning my Father's house into a shopping mall!" That's when his disciples remembered the Scripture, "Zeal for your house consumes me."

JOHN 2:13-17

Religion is easily and commonly commercialized. Each church needs repeated and vigorous temple-cleansings to restore it to its proper function as a center for prayer.

Where does the "zeal for your house" quotation come from?

Lord God of hosts, invade our cluttered churches, clogged with religious baggage, and do a good housecleaning among us so that there is room for the one thing needful, for prayer. Amen.

His Body as the Temple

But the Jews were upset. They asked, "What credentials can you present to justify this?" Jesus answered, "Tear down this Temple and in three days I'll put it back together." They were indignant: "It took forty-six years to build this Temple, and you're going to rebuild it in three days?" But Jesus was talking about his body as the Temple. Later, after he was raised from the dead, his disciples remembered he had said this. They then put two and two together and believed both what was written in Scripture and what Jesus had said.

JOHN 2:18-22

The body of Jesus took over the functions of the Jerusalem temple, centering attention on God's presence among his people, providing a focus for sacrifice and adoration, and best of all, showing forth the resurrection.

Compare this with 1 Corinthians 6:19.

Just as your body, Lord Jesus, was a temple, make mine also a temple — a place where your spirit dwells, a place to glorify God, a place for crucifixion and resurrection. Amen.

Inside and Out

During the time he was in Jerusalem, those days of the Passover Feast, many people noticed the signs he was displaying and, seeing they pointed straight to God, entrusted their lives to him. But Jesus didn't entrust his life to them. He knew them inside and out, knew how untrustworthy they were. He didn't need any help in seeing right through them.

JOHN 2:23-25

Jesus did not plot his course on the basis of popular opinion polls. The response of the crowds played no part in guiding his ministry. God provided the compass points for his journey.

At what seasons of the year does Passover come?

All the things that, in my naïveté, seem so important to me—acclaim, enthusiasm, success, acceptance—are on the periphery of your ministry, Lord Jesus. You march to a different drummer. Give me ears to hear that drum beat, too. Amen.

Born from Above

There was a man of the Pharisee sect, Nicodemus, a prominent leader among the Jews. Late one night he visited Jesus and said, "Rabbi, we all know you're a teacher straight from God. No one could do all the God-pointing, God-revealing acts you do if God weren't in on it." Jesus said, "You're absolutely right. Take it from me: Unless a person is born from above, it's not possible to see what I'm pointing to—to God's kingdom." "How can anyone," said Nicodemus, "be born who has already been born and grown up? You can't re-enter your mother's womb and be born again. What are you saying with this 'born-from-above' talk?" Jesus said, "You're not listening. Let me say it again. Unless a person submits to this original creation—the 'wind hovering over the water' creation, the invisible moving the visible, a baptism into a new life—it's not possible to enter God's kingdom. When you look at a baby, it's just that: a body you can look at and touch. But the person who takes shape within is formed by something you can't see and touch—the Spirit—and becomes a living spirit. So don't be so surprised when I tell you that you have to be 'born from above'—out of this world, so to speak."

JOHN 3:1-7

Birth is a sudden and violent transition from the womb to the world, from darkness to light, an explosion into humanity (the world of the flesh). New birth is the same transition into the reality of God.

Have you been born from above?

Spirit of God, breathe through my existence and bring new life to every part of it. Open my eyes to the light of salvation, make me conversant with the truth of faith; guide me in the growth of holiness, in Jesus Christ. Amen.

The Wind Blows This Way and That

"You know well enough how the wind blows this way and that. You hear it rustling through the trees, but you have no idea where it comes from or where it's headed next. That's the way it is with everyone 'born from above' by the wind of God, the Spirit of God."

JOHN 3:8

"Wind" and "spirit" are the same word in Greek. Neither is visible, but what they produce is visible. Will we believe that which we cannot see? We do it all the time with the wind; why don't we do it with the Spirit?

What do you know about the Spirit?

I look to you, O God, whom I do not see, to renew all that I do see. Even while I am immersed in the world of the senses, I put my trust in the world of the Spirit, where all strength, love, and redemption originate. Amen.

How Does This Happen?

Nicodemus asked, "What do you mean by this? How does this happen?" Jesus said, "You're a respected teacher of Israel and you don't know these basics? Listen carefully. I'm speaking sober truth to you. I speak only of what I know by experience; I give you witness only to what I have seen with my own eyes. There is nothing secondhand here, no hearsay. Yet instead of facing the evidence and accepting it, you procrastinate with questions. If I tell you things that are plain as the hand before your face and you don't believe me, what use is there in telling you of things you can't see, the things of God? No one has ever gone up into the presence of God except the One who came down from that Presence, the Son of Man. In the same way that Moses lifted the serpent in the desert so people could have something to see and then believe, it is necessary for the Son of Man to be lifted up—and everyone who looks up to him, trusting and expectant, will gain a real life, eternal life."

JOHN 3:9-15

There is much that we can understand about God's ways, but also much that we cannot. God's ways do not contradict our reason, but they do exceed our reason. The revelation that Christ ("who came down from that Presence") brings to us puts all the bits and pieces of our knowledge into a complete truth.

How does the reference to Moses help?

My questions and all knowledge barely make a dent in what I need to know, O Christ. Tell me all I need to know; show me what I need to do; complete my understanding with your revelation. Amen.

God Loved the World

"This is how much God loved the world: He gave his Son, his one and only Son. And this is why: so that no one need be destroyed; by believing in him, anyone can have a whole and lasting life."

JOHN 3:16

The verse is deservedly famous: from it we learn God's attitude toward us (love), his action among us (he gave his Son), and his purpose for us (lasting life). Everything we need to know about God — and all of it is good.

When did you first learn this verse?

"Love divine, all loves excelling, joy of heaven, to earth come down, fix in us Thy humble dwelling, all Thy faithful mercies crown! Jesus, Thou art all compassion, pure, unbounded love Thou art; visit us with Thy salvation, enter every trembling heart."[30] Amen.

The Crisis

"God didn't go to all the trouble of sending his Son merely to point an accusing finger, telling the world how bad it was. He came to help, to put the world right again. Anyone who trusts in him is acquitted; anyone who refuses to trust him has long since been under the death sentence without knowing it. And why? Because of that person's failure to believe in the one-of-a-kind Son of God when introduced to him. This is the crisis we're in: God-light streamed into the world, but men and women everywhere ran for darkness. They went for the darkness because they were not really interested in pleasing God. Everyone who makes a practice of doing evil, addicted to denial and illusion, hates God-light and won't come near it, fearing a painful exposure. But anyone working and living in truth and reality welcomes God-light so the work can be seen for the God-work it is."

JOHN 3:17-21

Judgment is not an arbitrary lashing out from a despotic deity; it is self-inflicted. It follows from the deliberate, conscious choice of darkness over light, of evil instead of good.

What is the crisis?

Thank you, gracious Father, for relieving me of fears but not of responsibility, for banishing my anxiety without robbing me of the dignity of decision, in the name of Jesus Christ, my Savior. Amen.

Baptizing at Aenon

After this conversation, Jesus went on with his disciples into the Judean countryside and relaxed with them there. He was also baptizing. At the same time, John was baptizing over at the Aenon near Salim, where water was abundant. This was before John was thrown into jail.

JOHN 3:22-24

The ministries of John and Jesus overlapped at Aenon, an obscure spring along the Jordan, in the magnificent practice of baptism—a sign of turning away from sin in repentance and evidence of turning toward God in faith. Baptism linked the two ministries so that nothing of value in John's ministry was lost in the full exercise of Jesus' ministry.

How is baptism an appropriate link?

Great God: such great acts of ministry! and in such ordinary, everyday places! Continue to do your great works in the kitchen and family room and bedrooms of my house, and among the neighbors on my street. In Jesus' name. Amen.

Off to the Sidelines

John's disciples got into an argument with the establishment Jews over the nature of baptism. They came to John and said, "Rabbi, you know the one who was with you on the other side of the Jordan? The one you authorized with your witness? Well, he's now competing with us. He's baptizing, too, and everyone's going to him instead of us." John answered, "It's not possible for a person to succeed—I'm talking about *eternal* success—without heaven's help. You yourselves were there when I made it public that I was not the Messiah but simply the one sent ahead of him to get things ready. The one who gets the bride is, by definition, the bridegroom. And the bridegroom's friend, his 'best man'—that's me—in place at his side where he can hear every word, is genuinely happy. How could he be jealous when he knows that the wedding is finished and the marriage is off to a good start? That's why my cup is running over. This is the assigned moment for him to move into the center, while I slip off to the sidelines."

JOHN 3:25-30

John, used to being at the center of attention, was ready, on signal, to step out of the spotlight into the shadows. All ministry is Christ's. There can be no competition or rivalry among people who are working God's will, even when they are working along different lines.

Do you think it was difficult for John to take second place?

Dear Jesus, teach me my place: as a servant, not a master; as the friend of the bridegroom, not the bridegroom; as a witness to the truth, not the truth itself. Amen.

From Above

"The One who comes from above is head and shoulders over other messengers from God. The earthborn is earthbound and speaks earth language; the heavenborn is in a league of his own. He sets out the evidence of what he saw and heard in heaven. No one wants to deal with these facts. But anyone who examines this evidence will come to stake his life on this: that God himself is the truth. The One that God sent speaks God's words. And don't think he rations out the Spirit in bits and pieces. The Father loves the Son extravagantly. He turned everything over to him so he could give it away—a lavish distribution of gifts. That is why whoever accepts and trusts the Son gets in on everything, life complete and forever! And that is also why the person who avoids and distrusts the Son is in the dark and doesn't see life. All he experiences of God is darkness, and an angry darkness at that."

JOHN 3:31-36

Jesus is not just a better version of Moses, or David, or Elijah—or John. He is different entirely: "from above." Jesus is not a word about God, but the very Word of God. His presence brings us into the fullness of God. In him we have not just a fragment of truth but the whole picture of redemption.

What is the difference between John and Jesus?

I receive of your fullness, O God in Christ. Increase my capacity to believe, to obey, and to enjoy. I will not be content with hand-me-down truth or secondhand faith. I want it fresh and whole. Amen.

Jacob's Well

Jesus realized that the Pharisees were keeping count of the baptisms that he and John performed (although his disciples, not Jesus, did the actual baptizing). They had posted the score that Jesus was ahead, turning him and John into rivals in the eyes of the people. So Jesus left the Judean countryside and went back to Galilee. To get there, he had to pass through Samaria. He came into Sychar, a Samaritan village that bordered the field Jacob had given his son Joseph. Jacob's well was still there. Jesus, worn out by the trip, sat down at the well. It was noon.

JOHN 4:1-6

For more than seven hundred years, racial hostility existed between Samaritans and Jews. But a thousand years before that, Jacob, a common ancestor, had dug a well from which they both drank. If we go back far enough in history, we find sources of a common heritage.

Name other Samaritans mentioned in the Bible.

Lord, plunge us in Jordan's baptismal stream; dig us a deep Samaritan well, waters to wash the guilt from our land; cleanse us and sing our peace. Amen.

The Generosity of God

A woman, a Samaritan, came to draw water. Jesus said, "Would you give me a drink of water?" (His disciples had gone to the village to buy food for lunch.) The Samaritan woman, taken aback, asked, "How come you, a Jew, are asking me, a Samaritan woman, for a drink?" (Jews in those days wouldn't be caught dead talking to Samaritans.) Jesus answered, "If you knew the generosity of God and who I am, you would be asking *me* for a drink, and I would give you fresh, living water."

JOHN 4:7-10

Jesus began the conversation by asking for something; he will end it by giving something. His asking is always preparatory to his giving. Our relationship with God changes radically when we realize the generous nature of his being; he does not harass us with petty requests but offers us a magnificent gift.

What is the "generosity of God"?

Deepen my sense of need, dear Christ. Enlarge my expectations of your gifts. Help me to see faith not so much as that which I give you, but as that which you give me—even eternal life. Amen.

Give Me This Water

The woman said, "Sir, you don't even have a bucket to draw with, and this well is deep. So how are you going to get this 'living water'? Are you a better man than our ancestor Jacob, who dug this well and drank from it, he and his sons and livestock, and passed it down to us?" Jesus said, "Everyone who drinks this water will get thirsty again and again. Anyone who drinks the water I give will never thirst—not ever. The water I give will be an artesian spring within, gushing fountains of endless life." The woman said, "Sir, give me this water so I won't ever get thirsty, won't ever have to come back to this well again!"

JOHN 4:11-15

Misunderstanding does not always prevent communication; sometimes, as in this case, it is a creative stimulus to pursue complete understanding. Jesus uses the physical as a basis of awakening desire for the spiritual.

Compare with Matthew 5:6.

Give me this water, Lord Jesus; satisfy my spirit at the deep well of eternal life, springing up abundantly. Let me drink of it daily and always, and never thirst again. Amen.

Worship in Spirit and Truth

He said, "Go call your husband and then come back." "I have no husband," she said. "That's nicely put: 'I have no husband.' You've had five husbands, and the man you're living with now isn't even your husband. . . ." "Oh, so you're a prophet! Well, tell me this: Our ancestors worshiped God at this mountain, but you Jews insist that Jerusalem is the only place for worship, right?" "Believe me, woman, . . . the time is coming—it has, in fact, come—when what you're called will not matter and where you go to worship will not matter. It's who you are and the way you live that count before God. Your worship must engage your spirit in the pursuit of truth. That's the kind of people the Father is out looking for: those who are simply and honestly *themselves* before him in their worship. God is sheer being itself—Spirit. Those who worship him must do it out of their very being, their spirits, their true selves, in adoration." The woman said, "I don't know about that. I do know that the Messiah is coming. When he arrives, we'll get the whole story." "I am he," said Jesus. "You don't have to wait any longer or look any further."

JOHN 4:16-21,23-26

The conversation intensified as the discussion moved from getting water out of a well to worshiping God. The woman was led into an awareness of her interior needs and of God's ultimate fulfillments.

What does this tell you about worship?

God, I don't want to get hung up on questions of the places for worship or the times to worship or the forms of worship: I want to worship, inwardly, ardently, and truly, and so discover you as the center of my life, in Jesus Christ. Amen.

It's Harvest Time!

Just then his disciples came back. They were shocked. They couldn't believe he was talking with that kind of a woman. No one said what they were all thinking, but their faces showed it. The woman took the hint and left. In her confusion she left her water pot. Back in the village she told the people, "Come see a man who knew all about the things I did, who knows me inside and out. Do you think this could be the Messiah?" And they went out to see for themselves. In the meantime, the disciples pressed him, "Rabbi, eat. Aren't you going to eat?" He told them, "I have food to eat you know nothing about." The disciples were puzzled. "Who could have brought him food?" Jesus said, "The food that keeps me going is that I do the will of the One who sent me, finishing the work he started. As you look around right now, wouldn't you say that in about four months it will be time to harvest? Well, I'm telling you to open your eyes and take a good look at what's right in front of you. These Samaritan fields are ripe. It's harvest time!"

JOHN 4:27-35

The description of the Samaritans as a field ripe for harvest must have been a surprise! The usual Jewish view was that they were no more than a vacant lot, filled with rubble. Jesus removed the blinders of prejudice from our eyes so that we can see truly.

Compare this with 1 Corinthians 3:6-9.

Forgive me, Lord, for rejecting people whom I suppose are not interested in your love and for avoiding others whom I think will revile your grace. Where I see a field of weeds you see a field ripe for harvest. Help me to see it your way. Amen.

Your Son Lives

Now he was back in Cana of Galilee, the place where he made the water into wine. Meanwhile in Capernaum, there was a certain official from the king's court whose son was sick. When he heard that Jesus had come from Judea to Galilee, he went and asked that he come down and heal his son, who was on the brink of death. Jesus put him off: "Unless you people are dazzled by a miracle, you refuse to believe." But the court official wouldn't be put off. "Come down! It's life or death for my son." Jesus simply replied, "Go home. Your son lives." The man believed the bare word Jesus spoke and headed home. On his way back, his servants intercepted him and announced, "Your son lives!" He asked them what time he began to get better. They said, "The fever broke yesterday afternoon at one o'clock." The father knew that that was the very moment Jesus had said, "Your son lives." That clinched it. Not only he but his entire household believed.

JOHN 4:46-53

The official believed before he saw. He did not require signs and wonders as a condition for his trust. He had nothing to sustain him on his trip homeward but the word of Jesus. He believed simply because Jesus spoke.

How far is it from Cana to Capernaum?

Jesus, speak the word that will put my faith in motion; then send me back to the sphere of my obedience and raise my expectations for the fulfillment of your promises. Amen.

I Don't Have Anybody

Soon another Feast came around and Jesus was back in Jerusalem. Near the Sheep Gate in Jerusalem there was a pool, in Hebrew called *Bethesda*, with five alcoves. Hundreds of sick people—blind, crippled, paralyzed—were in these alcoves. One man had been an invalid there for thirty-eight years. When Jesus saw him stretched out by the pool and knew how long he had been there, he said, "Do you want to get well?" The sick man said, "Sir, when the water is stirred, I don't have anybody to put me in the pool. By the time I get there, somebody else is already in." Jesus said, "Get up, take your bedroll, start walking." The man was healed on the spot. He picked up his bedroll and walked off.

JOHN 5:1-9

The sick man had been within sight of help throughout his illness. He knew he needed help; he knew help was available; but he couldn't help himself. Jesus helps those who can't help themselves.

What can't you do for yourself?

"I sought the Lord, and afterward I knew He moved my soul to seek Him, seeking me; it was not I that found, O Savior true; no, I was found of Thee."[31] Amen.

On a Level with God

The Jews stopped the healed man and said, "It's the Sabbath. You can't carry your bedroll around. It's against the rules." But he told them, "The man who made me well told me to. He said, 'Take your bedroll and start walking.'" They asked, "Who gave you the order to take it up and start walking?" But the healed man didn't know, for Jesus had slipped away into the crowd. A little later Jesus found him in the Temple and said, "You look wonderful! You're well! Don't return to a sinning life or something worse might happen." The man went back and told the Jews that it was Jesus who had made him well. That is why the Jews were out to get Jesus—because he did this kind of thing on the Sabbath. But Jesus defended himself. "My Father is working straight through, even on the Sabbath. So am I." That really set them off. The Jews were now not only out to expose him; they were out to *kill* him. Not only was he breaking the Sabbath, but he was calling God his own Father, putting himself on a level with God.

JOHN 5:10-18

Far from misunderstanding Jesus, his persecutors understood precisely what was involved: that Jesus, by healing on the Sabbath and calling God his Father, was the very presence of God among them. But they preferred to keep God at a distance.

How close to you do you want God?

I do this too, Lord: I acknowledge you, but want you to work only within the framework I have constructed; I believe in you, but get uncomfortable when you get involved in my affairs. Forgive me. Amen.

The Son Gives Life

So Jesus explained himself at length. "I'm telling you this straight. The Son can't independently do a thing, only what he sees the Father doing. What the Father does, the Son does. The Father loves the Son and includes him in everything he is doing. But you haven't seen the half of it yet, for in the same way that the Father raises the dead and creates life, so does the Son. The Son gives life to anyone he chooses."

JOHN 5:19-21

God the Father and God the Son, the God they could not see and the Christ they saw right before them, were, for all practical purposes, the same. The functions of the one were to audibly reveal the mind and visibly execute the will of the other.

What did he mean by "you haven't seen the half of it yet"?

I offer you my adoration and my obedience, Lord Jesus. By your life I discover redemption; in your words I find direction; through your resurrection I enjoy eternal life. All praise to your great name! Amen.

Honor the Son Equally

"Neither he nor the Father shuts anyone out. The Father handed all authority to judge over to the Son so that the Son will be honored equally with the Father. Anyone who dishonors the Son, dishonors the Father, for it was the Father's decision to put the Son in the place of honor. It's urgent that you listen carefully to this: Anyone here who believes what I am saying right now and aligns himself with the Father, who has in fact put me in charge, has at this very moment the real, lasting life and is no longer condemned to be an outsider. This person has taken a giant step from the world of the dead to the world of the living."

JOHN 5:22-24

It does no good to say that we honor God if we dishonor him in our actions. God is not a far-off idea that we venerate in pious moments; he is an actual presence that we respond to in the historical now of Jesus Christ.

How do you honor God?

"Blessing and honor and glory and power, wisdom and riches and strength evermore give ye to Him who our battle hath won, whose are the Kingdom, the crown, and the throne."[32] Amen.

The Dead Will Hear the Voice

"It's urgent that you get this right: The time has arrived—I mean right now!—when dead men and women will hear the voice of the Son of God and, hearing, will come alive. Just as the Father has life in himself, he has conferred on the Son life in himself. And he has given him the authority, simply because he is the Son of Man, to decide and carry out matters of Judgment. Don't act so surprised at all this. The time is coming when everyone dead and buried will hear his voice. Those who have lived the right way will walk out into a resurrection Life; those who have lived the wrong way, into a resurrection Judgment."

JOHN 5:25-29

The words of Jesus are not pious embroidery for religious pillows. The ministry of Jesus is radical and it is ultimate. It crashes the boundaries of death and summons all to a resurrection.

What happens at resurrection?

I hear thunder in your speech, O God; I see lightning in your acts. Storm through this soul of mine; wake the sleeping parts of me; raise the dead parts of me; stand me on my feet, alert and praising in your presence. Amen.

If You Believed Moses . . .

"I can't do a solitary thing on my own: I listen, then I decide. You can trust my decision because I'm not out to get my own way but only to carry out orders. If I were simply speaking on my own account, it would be an empty, self-serving witness. But an independent witness confirms me, the most reliable Witness of all. Furthermore, you all saw and heard John, and he gave expert and reliable testimony about me, didn't he? But my purpose is not to get your vote, and not to appeal to mere human testimony. I'm speaking to you this way so that you will be saved. John was a torch, blazing and bright, and you were glad enough to dance for an hour or so in his bright light. But the witness that really confirms me far exceeds John's witness. It's the work the Father gave me to complete. These very tasks, as I go about completing them, confirm that the Father, in fact, sent me. The Father who sent me, confirmed me. And you missed it. You never hear his voice, you never saw his appearance. There is nothing left in your memory of his Message because you do not take his Messenger seriously. You have your heads in your Bibles constantly because you think you'll find eternal life there. But you miss the forest for the trees. These Scriptures are all about *me*! And here I am, standing right before you, and you aren't willing to receive from me the life you say you want. I'm not interested in crowd approval. And do you know why? Because I know you and your crowds. I know that love, especially God's love, is not on your working agenda. I came with the authority of my Father, and you either dismiss me or avoid me. If another came, acting self-important, you would welcome him with open arms. How do you expect to get anywhere with God when you spend all your time jockeying for position with each other, ranking your rivals and ignoring God? But don't think I'm going to accuse you before my Father. Moses, in whom you put so much stock, is your accuser.

If you believed, really believed, what Moses said, you would believe me. He wrote of me. If you won't take seriously what *he* wrote, how can I expect you to take seriously what *I* speak?"

JOHN 5:30-47

Everything converges to authenticate Jesus as God's Christ: the ministry of John the Baptist (verses 33-35); the "very tasks," which anyone can observe and evaluate (verses 36-38); and the authoritative Scriptures (verses 39-47). The evidence is massive. Those who refuse to believe Jesus refuse on the grounds of sin, not logic.

What convinced you to believe in Jesus?

So far as I am able, Lord, I want to grasp the grand sweep of your reality and perceive each sharply etched detail of your presence. Use all the evidence—what others say about you, what you say about yourself, what the Scriptures say about you—to both enlarge and sharpen my faith. Amen.

Jesus Took the Bread

When Jesus looked out and saw that a large crowd had arrived, he said to Philip, "Where can we buy bread to feed these people?" He said this to stretch Philip's faith. He already knew what he was going to do. Philip answered, "Two hundred silver pieces wouldn't be enough to buy bread for each person to get a piece." One of the disciples—it was Andrew, brother to Simon Peter—said, "There's a little boy here who has five barley loaves and two fish. But that's a drop in the bucket for a crowd like this." Jesus said, "Make the people sit down." There was a nice carpet of green grass in this place. They sat down, about five thousand of them. Then Jesus took the bread and, having given thanks, gave it to those who were seated. He did the same with the fish. All ate as much as they wanted. When the people had eaten their fill, he said to his disciples, "Gather the leftovers so nothing is wasted." They went to work and filled twelve large baskets with leftovers from the five barley loaves.

JOHN 6:5-13

Jesus' feeding of the five thousand is a sign of both his intention and his ability to provide for us whatever we need. His care is all-inclusive. His power is unrestricted. Body and spirit are equally sustained by his command.

What material difference does Jesus make in your life?

In the meals I eat today, O God, I will receive your gifts. My food is evidence of what you make and what you give. Thank you for bread and fish, in Jesus' name. Amen.

Food That Sticks with You

In the evening his disciples went down to the sea, got in the boat, and headed back across the water to Capernaum. It had grown quite dark and Jesus had not yet returned. A huge wind blew up, churning the sea. They were maybe three or four miles out when they saw Jesus walking on the sea, quite near the boat. They were scared senseless, but he reassured them, "It's me. It's all right. Don't be afraid.". . . When [the crowd] found him back across the sea, they said, "Rabbi, when did you get here?" Jesus answered, "You've come looking for me not because you saw God in my actions but because I fed you, filled your stomachs—and for free. Don't waste your energy striving for perishable food like that. Work for the food that sticks with you, food that nourishes your lasting life, food the Son of Man provides. He and what he does are guaranteed by God the Father to last." To that they said, "Well, what do we do then to get in on God's works?" Jesus said, "Throw your lot in with the One that God has sent. That kind of a commitment gets you in on God's works."

JOHN 6:16-20,25-29

We can work for trivial ends or eternal ends. We can labor for that which passes away or for that which lasts forever. It is not a question of whether we work or not—we must work in either case—the question is, "For whom will we work?"

For whom do you work?

I put myself under your orders today, Lord Jesus. As I go to work, let me do everything in obedience to you and for the glory of your name, knowing that nothing is too slight or out of the way to be used to your glory. Amen.

Bread from Heaven

They waffled: "Why don't you give us a clue about who you are, just a hint of what's going on? When we see what's up, we'll commit ourselves. Show us what you can do. Moses fed our ancestors with bread in the desert. It says so in the Scriptures: 'He gave them bread from heaven to eat.'" Jesus responded, "The real significance of that Scripture is not that Moses gave you bread from heaven but that my Father is right now offering you bread from heaven, the *real* bread. The Bread of God came down out of heaven and is giving life to the world." They jumped at that: "Master, give us this bread, now and forever!"

JOHN 6:30-34

The people were right in connecting the manna in the wilderness with the feeding of the five thousand. But they were wrong in stopping there; by so doing they were missing the profound provisions by God to satisfy their soul's hunger.

What is the *real* bread Jesus was referring to?

God, I know that my entire life is surrounded by your providence and upheld by your mercy. I thank you for all that you give me, bread from the bakery and bread from heaven, satisfying my body and my spirit. Amen.

I Am the Bread of Life

Jesus said, "I am the Bread of Life. The person who aligns with me hungers no more and thirsts no more, ever. I have told you this explicitly because even though you have seen me in action, you don't really believe me. Every person the Father gives me eventually comes running to me. And once that person is with me, I hold on and don't let go. I came down from heaven not to follow my own whim but to accomplish the will of the One who sent me. This, in a nutshell, is that will: that everything handed over to me by the Father be completed—not a single detail missed—and at the wrap-up of time I have everything and everyone put together, upright and whole. This is what my Father wants: that anyone who sees the Son and trusts who he is and what he does and then aligns with him will enter *real* life, *eternal* life. My part is to put them on their feet alive and whole at the completion of time."

JOHN 6:35-40

Jesus is our staple product. Received into our lives, like bread, he is the basic stuff of life for us. In him the essential needs of the day are satisfied and the central purposes in eternity are fulfilled.

How is Jesus like bread?

"Break Thou the bread of life, dear Lord, to me, as Thou didst break the loaves beside the sea; beyond the sacred page I seek Thee, Lord; my spirit pants for Thee, O Living Word!"[33] Amen.

Don't Bicker

At this, because he said, "I am the Bread that came down from heaven," the Jews started arguing over him: "Isn't this the son of Joseph? Don't we know his father? Don't we know his mother? How can he now say, 'I came down out of heaven' and expect anyone to believe him?" Jesus said, "Don't bicker among yourselves over me. You're not in charge here. The Father who sent me is in charge. He draws people to me — that's the only way you'll ever come. Only then do I do my work, putting people together, setting them on their feet, ready for the End. This is what the prophets meant when they wrote, 'And then they will all be personally taught by God.' Anyone who has spent any time at all listening to the Father, really listening and therefore learning, comes to me to be taught personally — to see it with his own eyes, hear it with his own ears, from me, since I have it firsthand from the Father. No one has seen the Father except the One who has his Being alongside the Father — and you can see *me*."

JOHN 6:41-46

The conventional imagination reeled and rocked under the impact of Jesus' claim. The proclamation that God was actually present among them was staggering — and they staggered.

What Scripture does Jesus quote?

I bring such small-minded and cramped ideas to my encounters with you, Lord. And you come to me filling the air with a vast love and an immense grace! Stretch my mind to take in all that you are; enlarge my spirit to respond to all that you give, in Jesus Christ. Amen.

Down out of Heaven

"I'm telling you the most solemn and sober truth now: Whoever believes in me has real life, eternal life. I am the Bread of Life. Your ancestors ate the manna bread in the desert and died. But now here is Bread that truly comes down out of heaven. Anyone eating this Bread will not die, ever. I am the Bread—living Bread!—who came down out of heaven. Anyone who eats this Bread will live—and forever! The Bread that I present to the world so that it can eat and live is myself, this flesh-and-blood self."

JOHN 6:47-51

Life comes from above—not from around and not from within. Eternal salvation is a gift from God, not an accumulation of human virtue. We get what we need eternally by opening ourselves to God and receiving what he gives in Christ, not by trying to make it on our own.

What happened in the desert?

Dear Lord God, I don't want to live on the memory of old miracles, but experience fresh ones in faith. Draw me into the fullness of this day's grace in which you have new things to do in and through me, in Jesus. Amen.

How . . . ?

At this, the Jews started fighting among themselves: "How can this man serve up his flesh for a meal?" But Jesus didn't give an inch. "Only insofar as you eat and drink flesh and blood, the flesh and blood of the Son of Man, do you have life within you. The one who brings a hearty appetite to this eating and drinking has eternal life and will be fit and ready for the Final Day. My flesh is real food and my blood is real drink. By eating my flesh and drinking my blood you enter into me and I into you. In the same way that the fully alive Father sent me here and I live because of him, so the one who makes a meal of me lives because of me. This is the Bread from heaven. Your ancestors ate bread and later died. Whoever eats this Bread will live always." He said these things while teaching in the meeting place in Capernaum.

JOHN 6:52-59

Jesus does not answer questions, he asks them. He is not a puzzle for us to figure out, but the very life of God in the form we can receive it. Coming to Jesus is not entering a classroom but sitting down at a banquet.

Do your questions ever get in the way of your faith?

Father, your gifts are beyond my understanding; your life exceeds my ability to explain it. But explanations are not what I really want anyway. What I really want are deepened capacities to receive and enjoy, through Jesus Christ. Amen.

Tough Teaching

Many among his disciples heard this and said, "This is tough teaching, too tough to swallow." Jesus sensed that his disciples were having a hard time with this and said, "Does this throw you completely? What would happen if you saw the Son of Man ascending to where he came from? The Spirit can make life. Sheer muscle and willpower don't make anything happen. Every word I've spoken to you is a Spirit-word, and so it is life-making. But some of you are resisting, refusing to have any part in this." (Jesus knew from the start that some weren't going to risk themselves with him. He knew also who would betray him.) He went on to say, "This is why I told you earlier that no one is capable of coming to me on his own. You get to me only as a gift from the Father."

JOHN 6:60-65

The difficulty is not in what we must do, but what we must not do—namely, attempt to be gods or goddesses on our own. It is a lovely ambition and hard to give up. But until we do we cannot accept Christ as Lord and Savior.

Why do some still refuse to surrender?

Lord, you dash my fondest dreams—dreams of being in control of my life, dreams of controlling others. Then you give something far better—the vision of your lordship and redemption. Banish unbelief from my heart and grant, in your mercy, faith. Amen.

Do You Also Want to Leave?

After this a lot of his disciples left. They no longer wanted to be associated with him. Then Jesus gave the Twelve their chance: "Do you also want to leave?" Peter replied, "Master, to whom would we go? You have the words of real life, eternal life. We've already committed ourselves, confident that you are the Holy One of God." Jesus responded, "Haven't I handpicked you, the Twelve? Still, one of you is a devil!" He was referring to Judas, son of Simon Iscariot. This man—one from the Twelve!—was even then getting ready to betray him.

JOHN 6:66-71

Jesus trusts us with the big eternity-shaping decisions. He will not force us into virtue; he will not compel faith; he will not coerce us into discipleship. Following Jesus is a true and deep act of freedom.

What is the difference between Peter and Judas?

Lord Jesus Christ, keep me from wandering, from turning back, from quitting. By your grace "I've got my eye on the goal, where God is beckoning us onward—to Jesus" (Philippians 3:14). Amen.

His Brothers Didn't Believe

Later Jesus was going about his business in Galilee. He didn't want to travel in Judea because the Jews there were looking for a chance to kill him. It was near the time of Tabernacles, a feast observed annually by the Jews. His brothers said, "Why don't you leave here and go up to the Feast so your disciples can get a good look at the works you do? No one who intends to be publicly known does everything behind the scenes. If you're serious about what you are doing, come out in the open and show the world." His brothers were pushing him like this because they didn't believe in him either. Jesus came back at them, "Don't crowd me. This isn't my time. It's your time—it's *always* your time; you have nothing to lose. The world has nothing against you, but it's up in arms against me. It's against me because I expose the evil behind its pretensions. You go ahead, go up to the Feast. Don't wait for me. I'm not ready. It's not the right time for me." He said this and stayed on in Galilee.

JOHN 7:1-9

Unbelief is impatient with God's ways. The counsel of Jesus' brothers stemmed not from their trust in him but from their doubts about him. But Jesus will not be hurried, and he will not be pushed.

What kind of feast was Tabernacles?

Do it your way, Jesus, and in your time. Give me the gift of patience to wait, the gift of courage to persevere, and the gift of faith to believe that you do all things right. Amen.

I Didn't Make This Up

But later, after his family had gone up to the Feast, he also went. But he kept out of the way, careful not to draw attention to himself. The Jews were already out looking for him, asking around, "Where is that man?" There was a lot of contentious talk about him circulating through the crowds. Some were saying, "He's a good man." But others said, "Not so. He's selling snake oil." This kind of talk went on in guarded whispers because of the intimidating Jewish leaders. With the Feast already half over, Jesus showed up in the Temple, teaching. The Jews were impressed, but puzzled: "How does he know so much without being schooled?" Jesus said, "I didn't make this up. What I teach comes from the One who sent me. Anyone who wants to do his will can test this teaching and know whether it's from God or whether I'm making it up. A person making things up tries to make himself look good. But someone trying to honor the one who sent him sticks to the facts and doesn't tamper with reality. It was Moses, wasn't it, who gave you God's Law? But none of you are living it. So why are you trying to kill me?" The crowd said, "You're crazy! Who's trying to kill you? You're demon-possessed." Jesus said, "I did one miraculous thing a few months ago, and you're still standing around getting all upset, wondering what I'm up to. Moses prescribed circumcision—originally it came not from Moses but from his ancestors—and so you circumcise a man, dealing with one part of his body, even if it's the Sabbath. You do this in order to preserve one item in the Law of Moses. So why are you upset with me because I made a man's whole body well on the Sabbath? Don't be nitpickers; use your head—and heart!—to discern what is right, to test what is authentically right."

JOHN 7:10-24

The authority that everyone senses in Jesus' teaching is unaccountable in terms of human learning. He does not speak about God, giving secondhand information or leading an academic discussion; he speaks firsthand, confronting people with the personal will of God.

What healing did Jesus refer to?

Lord Jesus, draw me out of the crowd of spectators into the band of disciples, that I would not be among those who marvel and argue and discuss, but among those who listen and obey and believe. Amen.

I Come from Him

That's when some of the people of Jerusalem said, "Isn't this the one they were out to kill? And here he is out in the open, saying whatever he pleases, and no one is stopping him. Could it be that the rulers know that he is, in fact, the Messiah? And yet we know where this man came from. The Messiah is going to come out of nowhere. Nobody is going to know where he comes from." That provoked Jesus, who was teaching in the Temple, to cry out, "Yes, you think you know me and where I'm from, but that's not where I'm from. I didn't set myself up in business. My true origin is in the One who sent me, and you don't know him at all. I come from him—that's how I know him. He sent me here." They were looking for a way to arrest him, but not a hand was laid on him because it wasn't yet God's time. Many from the crowd committed themselves in faith to him, saying, "Will the Messiah, when he comes, provide better or more convincing evidence than this?"

JOHN 7:25-31

Jesus cannot be understood or explained in terms of his family life or his hometown origins. He can only be accounted for in terms of God's eternal plan of salvation and his gracious will to incarnation.

What signs had Jesus done?

Lead me deep into the sources of faith, O God. Take me beneath the surface so that I may see and understand the great and invisible foundation realities in your will and love. Amen.

What Is He Talking About?

The Pharisees, alarmed at this seditious undertow going through the crowd, teamed up with the high priests and sent their police to arrest him. Jesus rebuffed them: "I am with you only a short time. Then I go on to the One who sent me. You will look for me, but you won't find me. Where I am, you can't come." The Jews put their heads together. "Where do you think he is going that we won't be able to find him? Do you think he is about to travel to the Greek world to teach the Jews? What is he talking about, anyway: 'You will look for me, but you won't find me,' and 'Where I am, you can't come'?"

JOHN 7:32-36

Hostile opposition and skeptical rejection prevent understanding. Those who resist Jesus misunderstand Jesus. Faith, on the other hand, opens up the understanding, while obedience clarifies the revelation.

What was the reason the crowd was arrested?

I want a better understanding of your will for me, Lord; I want more light on your ways in my life. Direct me into the acts of obedience and the affirmations of faith that will show me what you are doing, in Jesus Christ. Amen.

Split in the Crowd

On the final and climactic day of the Feast, Jesus took his stand. He cried out, "If anyone thirsts, let him come to me and drink. Rivers of living water will brim and spill out of the depths of anyone who believes in me this way, just as the Scripture says." (He said this in regard to the Spirit, whom those who believed in him were about to receive. The Spirit had not yet been given because Jesus had not yet been glorified.) Those in the crowd who heard these words were saying, "This has to be the Prophet." Others said, "He is the Messiah!" But others were saying, "The Messiah doesn't come from Galilee, does he? Don't the Scriptures tell us that the Messiah comes from David's line and from Bethlehem, David's village?" So there was a split in the crowd over him. Some went so far as wanting to arrest him, but no one laid a hand on him.

JOHN 7:37-44

In their disagreement they agreed on one thing: Jesus was highly significant. He was either the best they had met, bringing to completion all God's ways with them, or he was a most dangerous impostor, who would, if permitted, lead people astray from God. No one dismissed him as a trifle.

Do you take Jesus seriously?

Father, keep my attention on the center — on eternal matters of creation and salvation, on the great realities of grace and truth, on the concerns for forgiveness and reconciliation, on decisions of faith — on Christ, in whose name I pray. Amen.

SEPTEMBER 17

Caught in the Act

The religion scholars and Pharisees led in a woman who had been caught in an act of adultery. They stood her in plain sight of everyone and said, "Teacher, this woman was caught red-handed in the act of adultery. Moses, in the Law, gives orders to stone such persons. What do you say?" They were trying to trap him into saying something incriminating so they could bring charges against him. Jesus bent down and wrote with his finger in the dirt. They kept at him, badgering him. He straightened up and said, "The sinless one among you, go first: Throw the stone." Bending down again, he wrote some more in the dirt. Hearing that, they walked away, one after another, beginning with the oldest. The woman was left alone. Jesus stood up and spoke to her. "Woman, where are they? Does no one condemn you?" "No one, Master." "Neither do I," said Jesus. "Go on your way. From now on, don't sin."

JOHN 8:3-11

Jesus takes sin more seriously than anyone, but he responds to it differently than most. He does not condemn, rejecting the sinner; he does not condone, ignoring the sin. He forgives.

Compare this with Romans 8:1.

Released from the tyranny of condemnation—by critics and by conscience—I find all things new, O Lord. Instill now strong habits of virtue in place of the sins to which I have become accustomed. Amen.

I Am the World's Light

Jesus once again addressed them: "I am the world's Light. No one who follows me stumbles around in the darkness. I provide plenty of light to live in."

JOHN 8:12

Light, God's creative work on the first day (see Genesis 1:3), is basic: It warms and illuminates. Jesus is light in this original sense — the condition for beginning life and the energy for continuing life.

Compare this with John 1:1-9.

"O gladsome light, O grace of God the Father's face, th'eternal splendor wearing; celestial, holy, blest, our Saviour Jesus Christ, joyful in Thine appearing."[34] Amen.

The Testimony of Two

The Pharisees objected, "All we have is your word on this. We need more than this to go on." Jesus replied, "You're right that you only have my word. But you can depend on it being true. I know where I've come from and where I go next. You don't know where I'm from or where I'm headed. You decide according to what you can see and touch. I don't make judgments like that. But even if I did, my judgment would be true because I wouldn't make it out of the narrowness of my experience but in the largeness of the One who sent me, the Father. That fulfills the conditions set down in God's Law: that you can count on the testimony of two witnesses. And that is what you have: You have my word and you have the word of the Father who sent me."

JOHN 8:13-18

Jesus' critics were tangled up in questions of procedure, anxious over the technicalities of the messianic evidence. But these questions cannot be decided by courtroom cross-examination: On their knees, in prayer to the Father, they would have realized the truth of Jesus' words and acts.

Why all the hostility?

Father in heaven, I thank you for the convincing clarity of your Christ. Help me this day to pay attention to what is right before my eyes, and so learn your truth and receive by faith the gift of eternal life in Jesus Christ. Amen.

If You Knew Me . . .

They said, "Where is this so-called Father of yours?" Jesus said, "You're looking right at me and you don't see me. How do you expect to see the Father? If you knew me, you would at the same time know the Father." He gave this speech in the Treasury while teaching in the Temple. No one arrested him because his time wasn't yet up.

JOHN 8:19-20

Much religious talk is a form of unbelief. These Pharisees were not trying to discover the truth in Jesus. Their questions were not a quest for salvation. If they had been seriously interested in the location of the Father, they would have recognized his presence in Jesus.

Do you ever ask questions in order to avoid the truth?

Lord, use the questions I raise about you to lead me directly and quickly into your presence, for it is not answers about you that I want but fellowship with you, in and through Jesus Christ. Amen.

Who Are You?

Then he went over the same ground again. "I'm leaving and you are going to look for me, but you're missing God in this and are headed for a dead end. There is no way you can come with me." The Jews said, "So, is he going to kill himself? Is that what he means by 'You can't come with me'?" . . . They said to him, "Just who are you anyway?" Jesus said, "What I've said from the start. I have so many things to say that concern you, judgments to make that affect you, but if you don't accept the trustworthiness of the One who commanded my words and acts, none of it matters. That is who you are questioning—not me but the One who sent me." They still didn't get it, didn't realize that he was referring to the Father. So Jesus tried again. "When you raise up the Son of Man, then you will know who I am—that I'm not making this up, but speaking only what the Father taught me. The One who sent me stays with me. He doesn't abandon me. He sees how much joy I take in pleasing him."

JOHN 8:21-22,25-29

Truth, the reality that is at the basis of all appearance, comes not so much by means of our intellect as through our obedience—"living out what I tell you" (John 8:31)—in personal relationship with Jesus. We find it not by reading books or by working in laboratories, but in following Jesus.

In what ways are you not free?

Free me, O Christ, from superstitions that confuse my mind, from misinformation that diverts me from obedience, from ignorance that pretends to be faith so that I may run unfettered in the way of your commandments. Amen.

Free Through and Through

Then Jesus turned to the Jews who had claimed to believe in him. "If you stick with this, living out what I tell you, you are my disciples for sure. Then you will experience for yourselves the truth, and the truth will free you." Surprised, they said, "But we're descendants of Abraham. We've never been slaves to anyone. How can you say, 'The truth will free you'?" Jesus said, "I tell you most solemnly that anyone who chooses a life of sin is trapped in a dead-end life and is, in fact, a slave. A slave is a transient, who can't come and go at will. The Son, though, has an established position, the run of the house. So if the Son sets you free, you are free through and through. I know you are Abraham's descendants. But I also know that you are trying to kill me because my message hasn't yet penetrated your thick skulls. I'm talking about things I have seen while keeping company with the Father, and you just go on doing what you have heard from your father."

JOHN 8:31-38

Sin promises what it cannot deliver: It promises freedom, a life of self-will unencumbered by God's will; it promises a future, a life of fulfillment, where personal desires are indulged and satisfied. But the promises are lies. Only God can provide freedom and a future for us.

Do you feel free?

"Make me a captive, Lord, and then I shall be free; force me to render up my sword, and I shall conqueror be."[35] Amen.

The Liar

They were indignant. "Our father is Abraham!" Jesus said, "If you were Abraham's children, you would have been doing the things Abraham did. And yet here you are trying to kill me, a man who has spoken to you the truth he got straight from God! Abraham never did that sort of thing. You persist in repeating the works of your father." They said, "We're not bastards. We have a legitimate father: the one and only God." "If God were your father," said Jesus, "you would love me, for I came from God and arrived here. I didn't come on my own. He sent me. Why can't you understand one word I say? Here's why: You can't handle it. You're from your father, the Devil, and all you want to do is please him. He was a killer from the very start. He couldn't stand the truth because there wasn't a shred of truth in him. When the Liar speaks, he makes it up out of his lying nature and fills the world with lies. I arrive on the scene, tell you the plain truth, and you refuse to have a thing to do with me."

JOHN 8:39-45

All the original and true relationships—with Abraham as our father in faith, with God as our father in love—are distorted by sin. We need supernatural help from the very start to recognize and respond to the truth in Jesus Christ.

How is Abraham your father?

God, I will not rely on my own understanding or trust in my own good intentions. Reveal your truth to me in Jesus and move me to faith by your Spirit so that I may live truly and freely. Amen.

Why Don't You Believe Me?

"Can any one of you convict me of a single misleading word, a single sinful act? But if I'm telling the truth, why don't you believe me? Anyone on God's side listens to God's words. This is why you're not listening—because you're not on God's side."

JOHN 8:46-47

The act of unbelief is not, as so many seem to think, a matter of an overactive, skeptical intellect. It is a stubborn and irrational act of will—a refusal to be in relationship with God.

What grounds did the Jews have for their unbelief?

You have assembled all the materials in creation to show your purposes, O God. You have revealed your very heart of love in Jesus to convince me of your goodness. All truth witnesses to you and all goodness leads to you. Hallelujah! Amen.

God Intends Something Glorious

The Jews then said, "That clinches it. We were right all along when we called you a Samaritan and said you were crazy — demon-possessed!" Jesus said, "I'm not crazy. I simply honor my Father, while you dishonor me. I am not trying to get anything for myself. God intends something gloriously grand here and is making the decisions that will bring it about. I say this with absolute confidence. If you practice what I'm telling you, you'll never have to look death in the face." At this point the Jews said, "Now we *know* you're crazy. Abraham died. The prophets died. And you show up saying, 'If you practice what I'm telling you, you'll never have to face death, not even a taste.' Are you greater than Abraham, who died? And the prophets died! Who do you think you are!" Jesus said, "If I turned the spotlight on myself, it wouldn't amount to anything. But my Father, the same One you say is your Father, put me here at this time and place of splendor. You haven't recognized him in this. But I have. If I, in false modesty, said I didn't know what was going on, I would be as much of a liar as you are. But I do know, and I am doing what he says. Abraham — your 'father' — with jubilant faith looked down the corridors of history and saw my day coming. He saw it and cheered." The Jews said, "You're not even fifty years old — and Abraham saw you?" "Believe me," said Jesus, "*I am who I am* long before Abraham was anything." That did it — pushed them over the edge. They picked up rocks to throw at him. But Jesus slipped away, getting out of the Temple.

JOHN 8:48-59

Jesus meets us, even when we are rude, where we are; but he will not cut down the garment of God's glory to fit our emaciated and underweight expectations. We are going to have to change, acquiring an appetite for a living God and a zest for eternity.

What don't you understand about Jesus?

Lord, I'm beginning to realize the way you work: You come to my level and attend to my difficulties so that I might come up to your level and share your glory. Thank you for your patience in starting with me where I am and your perseverance in taking me to where you are. Amen.

Who Sinned?

Walking down the street, Jesus saw a man blind from birth. His disciples asked, "Rabbi, who sinned: this man or his parents, causing him to be born blind?" Jesus said, "You're asking the wrong question. You're looking for someone to blame. There is no such cause-effect here. Look instead for what God can do. We need to be energetically at work for the One who sent me here, working while the sun shines. When night falls, the workday is over. For as long as I am in the world, there is plenty of light. I am the world's Light."

JOHN 9:1-5

Will we look on people in need—the ill and unfortunate—with accusing blame or with expectant hope? Are we interested in subjecting them to a moral dissection or in holding them up to the light of God's glory?

Note the similarities with John 1:4 and 8:12.

Lord Jesus, root out from my spirit the morbid curiosity that wants to pry into all the details of my neighbors' troubles, and replace it with a zestful interest in the glorious ways that you save and heal. Amen.

The Pool of Siloam

He said this and then spit in the dust, made a clay paste with the saliva, rubbed the paste on the blind man's eyes, and said, "Go, wash at the Pool of Siloam" (Siloam means "Sent"). The man went and washed — and saw. . . . They marched the man to the Pharisees. This day when Jesus made the paste and healed his blindness was the Sabbath. The Pharisees grilled him again on how he had come to see. He said, "He put a clay paste on my eyes, and I washed, and now I see." Some of the Pharisees said, "Obviously, this man can't be from God. He doesn't keep the Sabbath." Others countered, "How can a bad man do miraculous, God-revealing things like this?" There was a split in their ranks. They came back at the blind man, "You're the expert. He opened *your* eyes. What do you say about him?" He said, "He is a prophet." The Jews didn't believe it, didn't believe the man was blind to begin with. So they called the parents of the man now bright-eyed with sight. They asked them, "Is this your son, the one you say was born blind? So how is it that he now sees?" His parents said, "We know he is our son, and we know he was born blind. But we don't know how he came to see — haven't a clue about who opened his eyes. Why don't you ask him? He's a grown man and can speak for himself." (His parents were talking like this because they were intimidated by the Jewish leaders, who had already decided that anyone who took a stand that this was the Messiah would be kicked out of the meeting place. That's why his parents said, "Ask him. He's a grown man.") They called the man back a second time — the man who had been blind — and told him, "Give credit to God. We know this man is an imposter." He replied, "I know nothing about that one way or the other. But I know one thing for sure: I was blind . . . I now see." They said, "What did he do to you? How did he open your eyes?" "I've told you over and over and you haven't listened. Why do you want to hear it again? Are you so eager to become his disciples?" With that they jumped all over him. "*You* might be a disciple of that man, but we're disciples of Moses. We know for sure that God spoke to Moses, but we have no idea where this man even comes from." The man replied, "This is amazing! You claim to know nothing about him, but the fact is, he opened my eyes! It's well known that God isn't at the beck and call of sinners, but listens carefully to anyone who lives in reverence and does his will. That someone opened the eyes of a man born blind has never been heard of — ever. If this man didn't come from God, he wouldn't be able to do anything." They said, "You're nothing but dirt! How dare you take that tone with us!" Then they threw him out in the street.

JOHN 9:6-7,13-34

In obeying the directions of Jesus, the man experienced the light of Jesus. "All right knowledge of God is born of obedience."[36] Jesus is not a theory about light; he is light whom we experience by submitting to his touch and responding to his commands.

Do you know where the pool of Siloam is?

Touch me, command me, send me, Lord Jesus. Lead me out of the long night of my sin into the bright day of your salvation that I would live in your light and by your light. Amen.

And He Worshiped Him

Jesus heard that they had thrown him out, and went and found him. He asked him, "Do you believe in the Son of Man?" The man said, "Point him out to me, sir, so that I can believe in him." Jesus said, "You're looking right at him. Don't you recognize my voice?" "Master, I believe," the man said, and worshiped him.

JOHN 9:35-38

Excommunicated from the synagogue because of Christ, the man is now drawn into deep communion with God through Christ. His belief was not an item of information to which he gave assent, but a personal relationship to which he made a courageous commitment.

What is the relation between belief and worship?

I thank you, dear heavenly Father, for the work of Jesus: for the light he sheds on my way; for the ability he gives me to see the next step. As I follow in faith, lead me step by step into your fullness. Amen.

You're Calling Us Blind?

Jesus then said, "I came into the world to bring everything into the clear light of day, making all the distinctions clear, so that those who have never seen will see, and those who have made a great pretense of seeing will be exposed as blind." Some Pharisees overheard him and said, "Does that mean you're calling us blind?" Jesus said, "If you were really blind, you would be blameless, but since you claim to see everything so well, you're accountable for every fault and failure."

JOHN 9:39-41

Jesus is the light. In his presence, even the worst instance of blindness (the man born blind) is able to see; apart from his presence, even the best instance of enlightenment (the Pharisee) cannot see a thing.

How were the Pharisees blind?

"O God of Light, Thy Word, a lamp unfailing, shines through the darkness of our earthly ways, o'er fear and doubt, o'er black despair prevailing, guiding our steps to Thine eternal day."[37] *Amen.*

A Sheep Rustler!

"Let me set this before you as plainly as I can. If a person climbs over or through the fence of a sheep pen instead of going through the gate, you know he's up to no good—a sheep rustler! The shepherd walks right up to the gate. The gatekeeper opens the gate to him and the sheep recognize his voice. He calls his own sheep by name and leads them out."

JOHN 10:1-3

There is an immense amount of theft and violence in religion. Certain unscrupulous people, making concern for souls a pretext, pose as messengers of God but treat people as plunder, using them to get rich or to become powerful.

Have you ever been misled by a religious leader?

You have instructed me, Lord, to test the spirits. Sharpen my awareness of truth; give me wisdom to discern the falsehood that hides behind poses of piety and the mendacity that dresses in a cloak of religion. Amen.

Familiar with His Voice

"When he gets them all out, he leads them and they follow because they are familiar with his voice. They won't follow a stranger's voice but will scatter because they aren't used to the sound of it." Jesus told this simple story, but they had no idea what he was talking about.

JOHN 10:4-6

Just as sheep are familiar with the voice of their shepherd, so Christians are familiar with the voice of their Lord. Long association in a covenant of love substantiates faithfulness.

Read Psalm 23 for background.

In gratitude I listen to and obey your voice, Lord Jesus. Call me into paths of compassion and service, into ways of praise and joy, into places of hope and adoration. Amen.

I Am the Gate

So he tried again. "I'll be explicit, then. I am the Gate for the sheep. All those others are up to no good—sheep stealers, every one of them. But the sheep didn't listen to them. I am the Gate. Anyone who goes through me will be cared for—will freely go in and out, and find pasture."

JOHN 10:7-9

Jesus is a passageway. Going one way he leads us into the external world of creation, the visible realities of all things made in love and with purpose. Going the other way he leads us into the internal world of redemption, the invisible realities of grace and mercy which hold all things together.

What are some other functions of a door?

Through you, Lord Jesus Christ, I find my way out into a grand creation where everything is evidence of the Father's majesty, and I find my way into the Word where all is sustained and alive by the Spirit. Thank you for clear and easy access both ways. Amen.

More and Better

"A thief is only there to steal and kill and destroy. I came so they can have real and eternal life, more and better life than they ever dreamed of."

JOHN 10:10

Jesus does not need us to complete inadequacies in himself. He has no need to plunder our already depleted resources. He is already whole — and more. He overflows with life in himself and therefore is able to give to us, not take from us; to complete us, not exploit us.

What more do you want from God?

Fearlessly and hopefully I receive you, O Christ. Show me what I must do to live in health; lead me to the places where I live with meaning; provide me with the strength in which I can live exuberantly. Amen.

Good Shepherd

"I am the Good Shepherd. The Good Shepherd puts the sheep before himself, sacrifices himself if necessary."

JOHN 10:11

A persistent and influential image for God in Scripture is "shepherd." By it we understand God in Christ as strong and tender, courageous and intimate, provident and personal.

Read Ezekiel 34:7-16.

"The King of love my Shepherd is, whose goodness faileth never; I nothing lack if I am His and He is mine forever. In death's dark vale I fear no ill with Thee, dear Lord, beside me; Thy rod and staff my comfort still, Thy cross before to guide me."[38] Amen.

Hired Man

"A hired man is not a real shepherd. The sheep mean nothing to him. He sees a wolf come and runs for it, leaving the sheep to be ravaged and scattered by the wolf. He's only in it for the money. The sheep don't matter to him."

JOHN 10:12-13

There is nothing worse than people who use the spiritual needs of others to serve their own pride, who pretend to care for souls but only care for themselves. Jesus, in contrast, is unique and noble: completely without self-interest, wholly attendant on our eternal well-being.

What is a "hired man"?

Father, how I thank you for sending Jesus to be my shepherd: a Lord whom I can trust completely without the fear of being misled, a Savior upon whom I can rely absolutely, without the anxiety of being abandoned. Amen.

One Flock, One Shepherd

"I am the Good Shepherd. I know my own sheep and my own sheep know me. In the same way, the Father knows me and I know the Father. I put the sheep before myself, sacrificing myself if necessary. You need to know that I have other sheep in addition to those in this pen. I need to gather and bring them, too. They'll also recognize my voice. Then it will be one flock, one Shepherd."

JOHN 10:14-16

A good shepherd does not play favorites, concentrating his attention on a few and ignoring the many. The shepherd's concern and affection far exceed what a single fold of sheep, or a particular sheep, can experience or even be aware of.

Who are some of the "other sheep"?

Shepherd Christ, I hear your voice; how many others hear it too? As you lead me into green pastures and beside still waters, guide me into a fellowship of love with others who follow you. Amen.

I Lay Down My Life

"This is why the Father loves me: because I freely lay down my life. And so I am free to take it up again. No one takes it from me. I lay it down of my own free will. I have the right to lay it down; I also have the right to take it up again. I received this authority personally from my Father."

JOHN 10:17-18

Jesus picked up an earlier statement (see verse 11) and expanded it: His shepherding is voluntary and it is sacrificial. He is not a puppet pulled by the strings of fate: He chooses. And he is not a victim overwhelmed by malign forces: His sacrifice will conclude in a resurrection.

How did Jesus lay down his life?

Thank you, Lord Jesus, for going all the way for me, to the cross and to death, making there a "full, perfect, and sufficient sacrifice for the sins of the world"[39] and for my sins. Amen.

Tell Us Straight Out

A lot of them were saying, "He's crazy, a maniac—out of his head completely. Why bother listening to him?" But others weren't so sure: "These aren't the words of a crazy man. Can a 'maniac' open blind eyes?" They were celebrating Hanukkah just then in Jerusalem. It was winter. Jesus was strolling in the Temple across from Solomon's Porch. The Jews, circling him, said, "How long are you going to keep us guessing? If you're the Messiah, tell us straight out." Jesus answered, "I told you, but you don't believe. Everything I have done has been authorized by my Father, actions that speak louder than words. You don't believe because you're not my sheep. My sheep recognize my voice. I know them, and they follow me. I give them real and eternal life. They are protected from the Destroyer for good. No one can steal them from out of my hand."

JOHN 10:20-28

Those who insist on playing the leading part on center stage, using God only as background scenery and permitting him only a few off-stage whispers, will also complain that he does not speak clearly or act plainly. Of course not. But the fault is in their pride, not in his revelation.

What do you know about Hanukkah?

Lord, when others suggest detours through cloud-shadowed lanes of skepticism, direct me into the sunlit clarity of faith so that I may walk in your ways and not stumble, advance in your will and not wander, and come, finally, to your presence, where I will know even as I am known. Amen.

Under My Care

"The Father who put them under my care is so much greater than the Destroyer and Thief. No one could ever get them away from him. I and the Father are one heart and mind."

JOHN 10:29-30

Through Jesus we discover, by faith, absolute trust: That which we turn over to God is secure. He is not careless or absentminded with the precious treasure of our lives. God takes care of that which we give him.

What have you entrusted into the Father's care?

I commit myself and those I live with into your safekeeping, dear Father. Permit no evil to ruin our faith, no testing to damage our obedience, no unbelief to diminish our love, no anxieties to weaken our hope. You bought us with a great price; now keep us for eternity. Amen.

Blasphemy

Again the Jews picked up rocks to throw at him. Jesus said, "I have made a present to you from the Father of a great many good actions. For which of these acts do you stone me?" The Jews said, "We're not stoning you for anything good you did, but for what you said—this blasphemy of calling yourself God."

JOHN 10:31-33

Jesus' opponents were quite clear about one thing: Jesus was not merely a nice man running good-natured errands for the neighbors. He was either the very God or a blasphemer. Their accusation, while wrong, at least showed that they understood the issue.

Read Leviticus 24:16 for background.

Eternal God, I thank you for the mystery and miracle of your presence in Christ. You reveal yourself truly and share yourself wholly. Praise be to you, Father, Son, and Holy Spirit. Amen.

The Evidence Right Before
Your Eyes

Jesus said, "I'm only quoting your inspired Scriptures, where God said, 'I tell you — you are gods.' If God called your ancestors 'gods' — and Scripture doesn't lie — why do you yell, 'Blasphemer! Blasphemer!' at the unique One the Father consecrated and sent into the world, just because I said, 'I am the Son of God'? If I don't do the things my Father does, well and good; don't believe me. But if I am doing them, put aside for a moment what you hear me say about myself and just take the evidence of the actions that are right before your eyes. Then perhaps things will come together for you, and you'll see that not only are we doing the same thing, we *are* the same — Father and Son. He is in me; I am in him." They tried yet again to arrest him, but he slipped through their fingers. He went back across the Jordan to the place where John first baptized, and stayed there. A lot of people followed him over. They were saying, "John did no miracles, but everything he said about this man has come true." Many believed in him then and there.

JOHN 10:34-42

Jesus didn't say one thing and do another; he did what he said and said what he did. We can begin with either form of the revelation — the verbal or the visible, the words or the works — and be led to the same conclusion: This is the Christ of God.

How is Jesus like God?

God, thank you for giving me the whole picture in Jesus. Take everything I see and everything I hear and arrange it into a coherent, convincing revelation of your will to salvation. Amen.

Lazarus Is Sick

A man was sick, Lazarus of Bethany, the town of Mary and her sister Martha. This was the same Mary who massaged the Lord's feet with aromatic oils and then wiped them with her hair. It was her brother Lazarus who was sick. So the sisters sent word to Jesus, "Master, the one you love so very much is sick." When Jesus got the message, he said, "This sickness is not fatal. It will become an occasion to show God's glory by glorifying God's Son."

JOHN 11:1-4

No misfortune, it seems, is a disaster. Nothing is able, in itself, to separate us from God's purposes in Christ. And so Jesus' response to Lazarus' illness was both casual and confident. Even the things we call evil can be used by God to demonstrate his glory.

Why did the sisters send for Jesus?

You know, Lord, how faithless and nervous I am in the presence of illness and death: even though I know you are the great Physician; even though I know you are the resurrection and the life. Teach me to live in hope, responsive every moment to your glory. Amen.

Lazarus Died

Jesus loved Martha and her sister and Lazarus, but oddly, when he heard that Lazarus was sick, he stayed on where he was for two more days. After the two days, he said to his disciples, "Let's go back to Judea." They said, "Rabbi, you can't do that. The Jews are out to kill you, and you're going back?" Jesus replied, "Are there not twelve hours of daylight? Anyone who walks in daylight doesn't stumble because there's plenty of light from the sun. Walking at night, he might very well stumble because he can't see where he's going." He said these things, and then announced, "Our friend Lazarus has fallen asleep. I'm going to wake him up." The disciples said, "Master, if he's gone to sleep, he'll get a good rest and wake up feeling fine." Jesus was talking about death, while his disciples thought he was talking about taking a nap. Then Jesus became explicit: "Lazarus died. And I am glad for your sakes that I wasn't there. You're about to be given new grounds for believing. Now let's go to him." That's when Thomas, the one called the Twin, said to his companions, "Come along. We might as well die with him."

JOHN 11:5-16

Christ's love does not operate in the grooves of our expectation. He did not rush to heal Lazarus; he did not hurry to comfort Mary and Martha. But his measured, deliberate pace leads to an action that far exceeds our expectations.

Why did Jesus delay his coming?

"Unresting, unhasting, and silent as light, nor wanting, nor wasting, Thou rulest in might; Thy justice like mountains high soaring above, Thy clouds which are fountains of goodness and love."[40] Amen.

Resurrection and Life

When Jesus finally got there, he found Lazarus already four days dead. Bethany was near Jerusalem, only a couple of miles away, and many of the Jews were visiting Martha and Mary, sympathizing with them over their brother. Martha heard Jesus was coming and went out to meet him. Mary remained in the house. Martha said, "Master, if you'd been here, my brother wouldn't have died. Even now, I know that whatever you ask God he will give you." Jesus said, "Your brother will be raised up." Martha replied," I know that he will be raised up in the resurrection at the end of time." "You don't have to wait for the End. I am, right now, Resurrection and Life. The one who believes in me, even though he or she dies, will live. And everyone who lives believing in me does not ultimately die at all. Do you believe this?" "Yes, Master. All along I have believed that you are the Messiah, the Son of God who comes into the world."

JOHN 11:17-27

In Christ our destiny is not dissolution or annihilation or transmigration — or any of the other possibilities guessed by restless and curious minds — but actual, historical resurrection.

What is resurrection?

I believe in your resurrection, Lord Jesus Christ, and praise your marvelous and mighty name; and I believe in my resurrection, and wonder at your compassion and concern. You have the last word, and the last word is life, not death. Amen.

Jesus Wept

After saying this, she went to her sister Mary and whispered in her ear, "The Teacher is here and is asking for you." The moment she heard that, she jumped up and ran out to him. Jesus had not yet entered the town but was still at the place where Martha had met him. When her sympathizing Jewish friends saw Mary run off, they followed her, thinking she was on her way to the tomb to weep there. Mary came to where Jesus was waiting and fell at his feet, saying, "Master, if only you had been here, my brother would not have died." When Jesus saw her sobbing and the Jews with her sobbing, a deep anger welled up within him. He said, "Where did you put him?" "Master, come and see," they said. Now Jesus wept. The Jews said, "Look how deeply he loved him." Others among them said, "Well, if he loved him so much, why didn't he do something to keep him from dying? After all, he opened the eyes of a blind man."

JOHN 11:28-37

The power of Jesus did not isolate him from human pain or protect him from personal anguish. He participated in the emotions of death and grief completely. It is as important to realize his humanity ("Jesus wept") as it is to believe in his divinity ("I am . . . Resurrection and Life," verse 25) if we are to respond to the complete Christ.

Why did Jesus weep?

Because, Lord, nothing I experience is foreign to you and nothing I feel is strange to you, I am bold to draw near to the throne of grace to receive mercy and find grace in time of need (see Hebrews 4:16). Amen.

Lazarus, Come Out!

Then Jesus, the anger again welling up within him, arrived at the tomb. It was a simple cave in the hillside with a slab of stone laid against it. Jesus said, "Remove the stone." The sister of the dead man, Martha, said, "Master, by this time there's a stench. He's been dead four days!" Jesus looked her in the eye. "Didn't I tell you that if you believed, you would see the glory of God?" Then, to the others, "Go ahead, take away the stone." They removed the stone. Jesus raised his eyes to heaven and prayed, "Father, I'm grateful that you have listened to me. I know you always do listen, but on account of this crowd standing here I've spoken so that they might believe that you sent me." Then he shouted, "Lazarus, come out!" And he came out, a cadaver, wrapped from head to toe, and with a kerchief over his face. Jesus told them, "Unwrap him and let him loose."

JOHN 11:38-44

The same commanding voice that penetrated chaos and brought heaven and earth into being reached into the corruption of the grave and brought out a resurrection life.

What does this passage mean to you?

"I have a grave of sin. . . . Where Lazarus had been four days, I have been for fifty years. Why dost Thou not call me, as Thou didst him? I need Thy thunder, O my God! Thy music will not serve me."[41] Amen.

The Fragrance Filled the House

Six days before Passover, Jesus entered Bethany where Lazarus, so recently raised from the dead, was living. Lazarus and his sisters invited Jesus to dinner at their home. Martha served. Lazarus was one of those sitting at the table with them. Mary came in with a jar of very expensive aromatic oils, anointed and massaged Jesus' feet, and then wiped them with her hair. The fragrance of the oils filled the house. Judas Iscariot, one of his disciples, even then getting ready to betray him, said, "Why wasn't this oil sold and the money given to the poor? It would have easily brought three hundred silver pieces." He said this not because he cared two cents about the poor but because he was a thief. He was in charge of their common funds, but also embezzled them. Jesus said, "Let her alone. She's anticipating and honoring the day of my burial. You always have the poor with you. You don't always have me."

JOHN 12:1-8

The generous gift of Mary and the stingy complaint of Judas are placed in contrast. Mary used what she had to adore Jesus; Judas used Jesus to enrich himself. Mary was led into a life of devotion that was beautiful; Judas was posted as a warning against letting money get between us and God.

What are some other contrasts between Mary and Judas?

Lord, I place what I have in offering to you. And not just my money, but my life — my energies, my abilities and my goals. Let everything be fragrant in devotion to you. Amen.

A Grain of Wheat

The next day the huge crowd that had arrived for the Feast heard that Jesus was entering Jerusalem. They broke off palm branches and went out to meet him. And they cheered: "Hosanna! Blessed is he who comes in God's name! Yes! The King of Israel!" . . . There were some Greeks in town who had come up to worship at the Feast. They approached Philip . . . : "Sir, we want to see Jesus. Can you help us?" Philip went and told Andrew. Andrew and Philip together told Jesus. Jesus answered, "Time's up. The time has come for the Son of Man to be glorified. Listen carefully: Unless a grain of wheat is buried in the ground, dead to the world, it is never any more than a grain of wheat. But if it is buried, it sprouts and reproduces itself many times over. In the same way, anyone who holds on to life just as it is destroys that life. But if you let it go, reckless in your love, you'll have it forever, real and eternal. If any of you wants to serve me, then follow me. Then you'll be where I am, ready to serve at a moment's notice. The Father will honor and reward anyone who serves me."

JOHN 12:12-13,20-26

Jesus demonstrated, in word and act, how our lives are seed to be planted, not fruit to be preserved. When we realize the centrality of God in our lives, we are able to understand ourselves as gifts that we are free to share rather than as possessions that we must anxiously protect.

How did Jesus demonstrate this saying?

Where do I plant myself today, Lord? In what acts of love? In what routines of service? In what words of witness? I wait for your direction, ready to follow your lead. Amen.

A Voice

"Right now I am storm-tossed. And what am I going to say? 'Father, get me out of this'? No, this is why I came in the first place. I'll say, 'Father, put your glory on display.'" A voice came out of the sky: "I have glorified it, and I'll glorify it again." The listening crowd said, "Thunder!" Others said, "An angel spoke to him!" Jesus said, "The voice didn't come for me but for you. At this moment the world is in crisis. Now Satan, the ruler of this world, will be thrown out. And I, as I am lifted up from the earth, will attract everyone to me and gather them around me." He put it this way to show how he was going to be put to death. Voices from the crowd answered, "We heard from God's Law that the Messiah lasts forever. How can it be necessary, as you put it, that the Son of Man 'be lifted up'? Who is this 'Son of Man'?" Jesus said, "For a brief time still, the light is among you. Walk by the light you have so darkness doesn't destroy you. If you walk in darkness, you don't know where you're going. As you have the light, believe in the light. Then the light will be within you, and shining through your lives. You'll be children of light."

JOHN 12:27-36

It is all important that we realize the essential relation between Father and Son, between the heavenly voice and the earthly ministry, between the glorious will and purpose of God and the act of glory that is the death and resurrection of Jesus.

Compare this with Daniel 7:13-14.

Your acts are light, Lord Jesus, and your words are light — candescent marks that show the path of pilgrimage to God. Keep my eyes open to what you reveal and my heart obedient to what you will. Amen.

To Save the World

All these God-signs he had given them and they still didn't get it, still wouldn't trust him. . . . Jesus summed it all up when he cried out, "Whoever believes in me, believes not just in me but in the One who sent me. Whoever looks at me is looking, in fact, at the One who sent me. I am Light that has come into the world so that all who believe in me won't have to stay any longer in the dark. If anyone hears what I am saying and doesn't take it seriously, I don't reject him. I didn't come to reject the world; I came to save the world. But you need to know that whoever puts me off, refusing to take in what I'm saying, is willfully choosing rejection. The Word, the Word-made-flesh that I have spoken and that I am, *that* Word and no other is the last word. I'm not making any of this up on my own. The Father who sent me gave me orders, told me what to say and how to say it. And I know exactly what his command produces: real and eternal life. That's all I have to say. What the Father told me, I tell you."

JOHN 12:37,44-50

Jesus made a last, vigorous attempt to persuade the crowds — to break through the indifference of some and the fear of others. He is passionate and single-minded in his ministry of revealing God's will, drawing people to salvation and commanding eternal life.

How does judgment get set in motion?

Save me, Lord Jesus Christ. Expose my sin and lead me to the place of forgiveness; heal my faithlessness and make me healthy with love; convert my rebellion and train me in persevering discipleship. Amen.

You Wash My Feet?

Just before the Passover Feast, Jesus knew that the time had come to leave this world to go to the Father. Having loved his dear companions, he continued to love them right to the end. It was suppertime. The Devil by now had Judas, son of Simon the Iscariot, firmly in his grip, all set for the betrayal. Jesus knew that the Father had put him in complete charge of everything, that he came from God and was on his way back to God. So he got up from the supper table, set aside his robe, and put on an apron. Then he poured water into a basin and began to wash the feet of the disciples, drying them with his apron. When he got to Simon Peter, Peter said, "Master, *you* wash *my* feet?" Jesus answered, "You don't understand now what I'm doing, but it will be clear enough to you later."

JOHN 13:1-7

For some people, accepting an act of ministry is more difficult than offering it, for when another assists us our dependence, weakness, and need are admitted. When Peter abandoned his pose as the all-sufficient self-made man and received Jesus' ministry, he acted by faith.

Is it difficult for you to accept help?

I know, Lord, that it is pride that wants to assert absolute independence and be free from all obligations. I would like never to have to ask anybody for anything, not even you. Forgive my self-righteousness and clothe me in your righteousness. Amen.

Entirely Clean

Peter persisted, "You're not going to wash my feet—ever!" Jesus said, "If I don't wash you, you can't be part of what I'm doing." "Master!" said Peter. "Not only my feet, then. Wash my hands! Wash my head!"

JOHN 13:8-9

The acts of ministry that impinge upon us in Christ are not tokens, external trivialities that may or may not remind us of something important; they are sacramental signs: evidence of a deep and thoroughgoing inward transformation.

Compare this with 1 John 1:9.

Cleanse me, Christ. Wash the stain of sin from my soul, blow the dust of doubt from my mind, wipe the dirt of evil from my spirit: I long to be perfectly whole. Amen.

Not Every One of You

Jesus said, "If you've had a bath in the morning, you only need your feet washed now and you're clean from head to toe. My concern, you understand, is holiness, not hygiene. So now you're clean. But not every one of you." (He knew who was betraying him. That's why he said, "Not every one of you.")

JOHN 13:10-11

Judas submitted his feet to Jesus' washing, but withheld his heart. The water never got beneath his skin. Christ's cleansing requires inner acceptance.

Why did Judas betray Jesus?

"Generous in love—God, give grace! Huge in mercy—wipe out my bad record. Scrub away my guilt, soak out my sins in your laundry" (Psalm 51:1-2). Amen.

A Pattern

After he had finished washing their feet, he took his robe, put it back on, and went back to his place at the table. Then he said, "Do you understand what I have done to you? You address me as 'Teacher' and 'Master,' and rightly so. That is what I am. So if I, the Master and Teacher, washed your feet, you must now wash each other's feet. I've laid down a pattern for you. What I've done, you do. I'm only pointing out the obvious."

John 13:12-15

Jesus' life is not only a unique and indispensable ministry — the one we need to reveal God to us and to reconcile us to God — but our common example, the model from which we learn to live truly and rightly.

What act of service will you do today?

Lord Jesus, you couldn't have made it any more clear; you couldn't have said it more plainly. Why do I have so much difficulty following your example? Pride gets in the way. Overcome my selfishness and train me in devout service. Amen.

A Blessed Life

"A servant is not ranked above his master; an employee doesn't give orders to the employer. If you understand what I'm telling you, act like it—and live a blessed life."

John 13:16-17

Knowing is not enough. Understanding must be completed by obedience. What the head knows and the heart feels must be coordinated with what the hands do and where the feet go.

How do you express your faith in action?

Servant Christ, you show me how to serve; you command me to serve; you bless me as I serve. I praise you for the servant way, its joy and its glory. Amen.

You Will Believe

"I'm not including all of you in this. I know precisely whom I've selected, so as not to interfere with the fulfillment of this Scripture: 'The one who ate bread at my table turned on his heel against me.' I'm telling you all this ahead of time so that when it happens you will believe that I am who I say I am."

JOHN 13:18-19

The way Jesus turned Judas' betrayal, the Jewish trial, and the Roman crucifixion into acts of atonement and redemption is as powerful an incentive to believe as the positive acts of revelation in which he shows his glory.

What Scripture does Jesus quote?

Even more impressive, Lord, than the signs that show your life and your love is the way you use the malice of evil men to do the work of salvation: "Instead of smoldering rage — God-praise!" (Psalm 76:10). Amen.

Receiving

"Make sure you get this right: Receiving someone I send is the same as receiving me, just as receiving me is the same as receiving the One who sent me."

JOHN 13:20

We take what God gives through the servant whom he sends. The act of ministry is for our salvation whether or not the minister is to our taste. We cannot be snobbish; we must not be fussy. Receive.

Whom has God sent to you?

Father, you send messengers and provide ministries, and I receive. Help me to be hospitable and open to all who come, grateful and accepting of each who speaks in your name, for "some have extended hospitality to angels without ever knowing it!" (Hebrews 13:2). Amen.

Who?

After he said these things, Jesus became visibly upset, and then he told them why. "One of you is going to betray me." The disciples looked around at one another, wondering who on earth he was talking about. One of the disciples, the one Jesus loved dearly, was reclining against him, his head on his shoulder. Peter motioned to him to ask who Jesus might be talking about. So, being the closest, he said, "Master, who?" Jesus said, "The one to whom I give this crust of bread after I've dipped it." Then he dipped the crust and gave it to Judas, son of Simon the Iscariot. As soon as the bread was in his hand, Satan entered him. "What you must do," said Jesus, "do. Do it and get it over with." No one around the supper table knew why he said this to him. Some thought that since Judas was their treasurer, Jesus was telling him to buy what they needed for the Feast, or that he should give something to the poor. Judas, with the piece of bread, left. It was night.

JOHN 13:21-30

How a person who had been at Jesus' side for so long, who had experienced his virtue and enjoyed his blessing, could deliberately plot his betrayal escapes logic. All, though, who are not self-deceived know their own capacity for the entire range of sin.

Which disciple was called "the one Jesus loved dearly"?

"O break, O break, hard heart of mine! Thy weak self-love and guilty pride His Pilate and His Judas were: Jesus our Lord, is crucified!"[42] Amen.

Glorified

When he had left, Jesus said, "Now the Son of Man is seen for who he is, and God seen for who he is in him. The moment God is seen in him, God's glory will be on display. In glorifying him, he himself is glorified—glory all around!"

JOHN 13:31-32

Glory—an important word in John's gospel—refers to the open display of God's good will, his loving salvation, his redeeming purpose. As Judas was swallowed up in the night, Jesus emphasized this theme to focus attention on what God was doing, not on what Judas did.

How many times is glory (in any form of the word) mentioned here?

You know, God, my fondness for eavesdropping on the gossip of the wicked and entertaining in my heart tales of sin when I should be absorbed in the dramatic story of salvation in Jesus. Help me to pay attention to what is really important—your works and your words. Amen.

A New Command

"Let me give you a new command: Love one another. In the same way I loved you, you love one another."

JOHN 13:34

Love is defined ("in the same way I loved you") and commanded. It has nothing to do with soupy feelings, and it is not an optional feature for attachment to basic religion if we happen to be inclined in that direction. It is what Christ did and what we must do.

What is new about love?

Jesus Christ, your words have been flattened by so many repetitions and dulled by so many hypocrisies that I hear them as neither new nor commanding. By your Spirit restore fresh, explosive force to the words so that I may hear with zest and obey with zeal. Amen.

This Is How . . .

"This is how everyone will recognize that you are my disciples—when they see the love you have for each other."

JOHN 13:35

A most surprising identification card! Not "if we hold the right doctrine"; not "if we have membership in the right church"; not "if we work hard for justice"; not "if we are knowledgeable in Scripture"; not "if we diligently and successfully use our talents." The only Christ-authorized mark of discipleship is love for one another.

Is this the way others recognize you?

Dear Jesus, you have showed me how to love you; you have commanded me to love; you are in and with me to love. Develop in me a deep, consistent, and mature love for others. Amen.

Deny Me Three Times

Simon Peter asked, "Master, just where are you going?" Jesus answered, "You can't now follow me where I'm going. You will follow later." "Master," said Peter, "why can't I follow now? I'll lay down my life for you!" "Really? You'll lay down your life for me? The truth is that before the rooster crows, you'll deny me three times."

JOHN 13:36-38

Among the twelve, Peter and Judas were the conspicuous sinners. But the contrasts between them were substantial: Judas's betrayal was calculated; Peter's denial was spontaneous. Judas's sin plunged him into the despair of outer darkness; Peter's sin brought him to a godly sorrow that worked repentance. No sin must separate us from God; any sin can.

In what other ways do Judas and Peter differ?

Father in heaven, I make many naive promises and brave-sounding resolves. Much of it is sounding brass and clashing cymbals. I start out expecting your congratulations and end up needing your compassion. Receive me in mercy and forgive me for the sake of Jesus Christ. Amen.

Trust

"Don't let this throw you. You trust God, don't you? Trust me."

JOHN 14:1

The evening before his crucifixion, Jesus had an extended conversation with his disciples (see John 14–17). His purpose was to prepare them for a courageous act of belief—to trust in him even when it looked like everything was falling apart.

What troubles do you face?

God, you well know how the troubles in the world and the troubles in my heart gang up on me and threaten to defeat me. I reaffirm my trust in your strong presence and wait on you to renew my strength, through Jesus Christ. Amen.

In My Father's Home

"There is plenty of room for you in my Father's home. If that weren't so, would I have told you that I'm on my way to get a room ready for you? And if I'm on my way to get your room ready, I'll come back and get you so you can live where I live. And you already know the road I'm taking."

JOHN 14:2-4

Heaven will not be a vast spectacular country to visit as a tourist; it is a place where we will have a home and dwell as citizens. Jesus' words make heaven as specific and sure as any dwelling place we know on earth.

Why is heaven important?

Lord Jesus, when I worry about the future, harboring anxieties about health or money or family, revive these words in my memory and refresh me with the knowledge that the future is where you are getting things ready for me. Amen.

We Have No Idea

Thomas said, "Master, we have no idea where you're going. How do you expect us to know the road?" Jesus said, "I am the Road, also the Truth, also the Life. No one gets to the Father apart from me. If you really knew me, you would know my Father as well. From now on, you do know him. You've even seen him!"

JOHN 14:5-7

Thomas's question defines our quest; Jesus' answer maps out our journey. But Jesus does more than give us a map. He not only plainly and personally shows us the way to God, he actually takes us to him.

Why is Jesus important?

Christ my Savior, how much motion I waste, how much needless searching I do, when all I have to do is follow you, listen to you, and let you live your eternal life in me. "I'll run the course you lay out for me if you'll just show me how" (Psalm 119:32). Amen.

Show Us the Father

Philip said, "Master, show us the Father; then we'll be content." "You've been with me all this time, Philip, and you still don't understand? To see me is to see the Father. So how can you ask, 'Where is the Father?' Don't you believe that I am in the Father and the Father is in me? The words that I speak to you aren't mere words. I don't just make them up on my own. The Father who resides in me crafts each word into a divine act."

JOHN 14:8-10

Philip's question was a search for God; Jesus' answer ended the search: God is in Christ. God is historically revealed and defined. Speculations about God are over. Now the question is, "Will you believe in him, or not?"

What is your question for God?

Sometimes, Lord, I ask questions just to put off going to work as your disciple. I wonder if Philip was doing that? Like him, I know more than enough already — help me to put it into practice in active faith in Jesus Christ, your Son, my Savior. Amen.

Words . . . Works

"Believe me: I am in my Father and my Father is in me. If you can't believe that, believe what you see—these works."

JOHN 14:11

We can take the meaning of Jesus' words, or we can observe the evidence of his works. We can listen to him, or we can watch him. Both the words and the works lead to the same conclusion: Jesus reveals God to us.

Do you place more value on words or works?

Lord Jesus Christ, I thank you for your words—clear and convincing; and I thank you for your works—plain and definitive. Thank you for a complete revelation and a whole salvation. Amen.

Greater Things

"The person who trusts me will not only do what I'm doing but even greater things, because I, on my way to the Father, am giving you the same work to do that I've been doing. You can count on it."

JOHN 14:12

God does not want us to be docile followers of Jesus, so overawed by him that we never attempt anything but pale imitations of his works. He intends people full of initiative, expanding in countless ways the ministry of redemptive love he launched.

What are some of the "greater things"?

Father in heaven, it is hard for me to think of doing greater things than your Son. What those things are is your business; the willingness to shed my lazy timidity and start believing and praying after the manner of Jesus is mine. I ask for help to do it faithfully. In Jesus' name. Amen.

Request

"From now on, whatever you request along the lines of who I am and what I am doing, I'll do it. That's how the Father will be seen for who he is in the Son. I mean it. Whatever you request in this way, I'll do."

JOHN 14:13-14

Too often we ask for things we don't need from people who can't supply our needs. Jesus' generous invitation, "Request," involves us in receiving the gifts God has for us, doing ministries to which he calls us, and experiencing the grace and mercy by which he completes us.

What will you ask God for?

God, instead of asking for many things I'll never need, from merchants and entertainers and friends, I will ask you for the few things I need eternally—light to take the next step in faith, grace to persevere for another day, forgiveness that changes sin to salvation. Amen.

If

"If you love me, show it by doing what I've told you."

JOHN 14:15

Obedience is rooted in love, not fear; it is activated by affection, not by force. Keeping the commandments, for Christians, is not dull rule-keeping but passionate love-making. Each commandment is a channel for expressing and sharing God's goodness.

What are your favorite commandments?

Thank you for the commandments, God—for so many clear-cut and convenient ways to express my love for you and for others. "Seven times each day I stop and shout praises for the way you keep everything running right" (Psalm 119:164). Amen.

Another Friend

"I will talk to the Father, and he'll provide you another Friend so that you will always have someone with you. This Friend is the Spirit of Truth. The godless world can't take him in because it doesn't have eyes to see him, doesn't know what to look for. But you know him already because he has been staying with you, and will even be *in* you!"

JOHN 14:16-17

When we are puzzled in life, we consult wiser, more experienced people—counselors, friends. Their sympathetic insight clarifies and encourages. The Holy Spirit is God-living-in-us to do just such work.

What has the Counselor clarified for you?

God, why am I running to the so-called wise men of this world every time I have a problem, when you have provided me with a resident Friend, even your Holy Spirit? I ought to be consulting you; I will consult you! In Jesus' name. Amen.

Orphaned

"I will not leave you orphaned. I'm coming back. In just a little while the world will no longer see me, but you're going to see me because I am alive and you're about to come alive."

JOHN 14:18-19

The desolate separation between human beings and God is overcome by Jesus. He bridges the chasm between our sin and the Father's holiness. The result is a new shared life between Creator and creature, animated by love.

How does God keep his promise?

How faithfully you keep your promises, God! Your presence drives out loneliness, your love banishes emptiness, your commands cure my aimlessness. Thank you for continuing to be with me in Jesus, through the Holy Spirit. Amen.

In

"In just a little while the world will no longer see me, but you're going to see me because I am alive and you're about to come alive. At that moment you will know absolutely that I'm in my Father, and you're in me, and I'm in you. The person who knows my commandments and keeps them, that's who loves me. And the person who loves me will be loved by my Father, and I will love him and make myself plain to him."

JOHN 14:19-21

"In" is the preposition of intimacy and one of the most important words in the gospel. It is later picked up by Paul and used in his famous formula "in Christ." Jesus sets us in a relationship of intimacy with himself by which we experience the fullness of God.

Read Ephesians 2:13.

Jesus, I know that you will not leave me empty or orphaned. I thank you for the promise of your presence. Invade, invigorate, inspire by your Spirit. Amen.

If Anyone Loves Me . . .

Judas (not Iscariot) said, "Master, why is it that you are about to make yourself plain to us but not to the world?" "Because a loveless world," said Jesus, "is a sightless world. If anyone loves me, he will carefully keep my word and my Father will love him—we'll move right into the neighborhood! Not loving me means not keeping my words. The message you are hearing isn't mine. It's the message of the Father who sent me."

JOHN 14:22-24

Judas tried to understand why God treats Christians differently from others. Jesus answered that he doesn't. The difference is in the love that responds to God's words and creates hospitable conditions for God's dwelling in us: "my heart—Christ's home."[43]

How does love change your relation with God?

God, I have such shallow, Hollywoodish ideas of love. I keep thinking it has to do with sunsets and soft music. You have something different in mind—not a feeling about you, but a decision for you, a decision that produces obedience and accepts your presence in Jesus Christ. Teach me such a love, for Jesus' sake. Amen.

Make Everything Plain

"I'm telling you these things while I'm still living with you. The Friend, the Holy Spirit whom the Father will send at my request, will make everything plain to you. He will remind you of all the things I have told you. I'm leaving you well and whole."

JOHN 14:25-26

When someone leaves us, we are poorer for his absence; when Jesus left his disciples, they were suddenly richer. They had, instead of the physical form of Jesus with them, the Holy Spirit in them.

What has the Holy Spirit taught you?

Holy Spirit, bring to my remembrance the words of Jesus that I may not be without guidance as I follow him, nor without knowledge as I speak of him, nor without peace as I trust in him. Amen.

N O V E M B E R   1 5

Peace

"That's my parting gift to you. Peace. I don't leave you the way you're used to being left—feeling abandoned, bereft. So don't be upset. Don't be distraught."

JOHN 14:27

The world's way to get peace is to eliminate that which disturbs; God's way is to restore the unruly. The world's way to get peace is to say, "Shut up, I don't want to hear it anymore"; the Lord's way is to say, "Step out of the traffic! Take a long, loving look at me, your High God" (Psalm 46:10). The world's peace is a precarious house of cards; God's peace is a cosmic wholeness.

How would you define peace?

"Thy mighty name salvation is, and keeps my happy soul above: comfort it brings, and power, and peace, and joy, and everlasting love: to me, with Thy great name, are given pardon and holiness and heaven."[44] Amen.

On My Way to the Father

"You've heard me tell you, 'I'm going away, and I'm coming back.' If you loved me, you would be glad that I'm on my way to the Father because the Father is the goal and purpose of my life. I've told you this ahead of time, before it happens, so that when it does happen, the confirmation will deepen your belief in me."

JOHN 14:28-29

The disciples' love for Jesus was already strong. Jesus now leads them to extend that love to the Father. As Jesus goes to the Father, he leads them (and us) through their devotion to the Father also.

Why does Jesus go away?

Father in heaven, I rejoice in these words of your son. They encourage and hearten me. Believing in him I also want to follow him until I finally arrive where he leads me — in your presence. Amen.

Let's Go

"I'll not be talking with you much more like this because the chief of this godless world is about to attack. But don't worry—he has nothing on me, no claim on me. But so the world might know how thoroughly I love the Father, I am carrying out my Father's instructions right down to the last detail. Get up. Let's go. It's time to leave here."

JOHN 14:30-31

Jesus had many things to say to his friends; he also had many things to show them: Jesus' words were completed in his actions. The leisurely hours of discourse led into strenuous hours of trial and crucifixion.

Are you as ready to go as to talk?

Jesus Christ, I like the way in which all your words become acts of faith and obedience. I like to ponder your words; I also like participating in your passion. Thank you for both the truths that give meaning and the commands that shape purpose in my life with you. Amen.

I Am the Real Vine

"I am the Real Vine and my Father is the Farmer. He cuts off every branch of me that doesn't bear grapes. And every branch that is grape-bearing he prunes back so it will bear even more. You are already pruned back by the message I have spoken."

JOHN 15:1-3

Jesus is not a decorative shrub, useful for giving an aesthetic religious touch to life. He is not available to be arranged in a bouquet to delight us. He is life itself, its very center — the vine.

Compare this with Isaiah 5:1-7.

God, my habit is to think of myself as the vine with others branching off of me. How wrong! Jesus is the vine, and I am a branch on him. Do whatever needs to be done, Father, to make this vine-branch connection vigorous and healthy, in Jesus' name. Amen.

Live in Me

"Live in me. Make your home in me just as I do in you. In the same way that a branch can't bear grapes by itself but only by being joined to the vine, you can't bear fruit unless you are joined with me."

JOHN 15:4

It is hopeless to try to be a human being apart from Christ—just as it is impossible for a branch severed from its vine to bear grapes. The basic choice we all make is whether we will get it on our own, or live in Christ, the vine.

How do you live in Christ?

Lord, your invitation is insistently gracious. It is quite plain that you don't leave any middle ground for casual, occasional, more-or-less religious visits between us. It is either live in him or be cast forth. I choose to live in you, even as you have invited and commanded. Amen.

Abundant Harvest

"I am the Vine, you are the branches. When you're joined with me and I with you, the relation intimate and organic, the harvest is sure to be abundant. Separated, you can't produce a thing. Anyone who separates from me is deadwood, gathered up and thrown on the bonfire. But if you make yourselves at home with me and my words are at home in you, you can be sure that whatever you ask will be listened to and acted upon. This is how my Father shows who he is—when you produce grapes, when you mature as my disciples."

JOHN 15:5-8

The invitation to ask whatever you will is linked to the goal to bear "abundant" harvest. When we live in Christ, our prayers cease to be disguised efforts to increase personal possessions and power and become the means of being increased in Christ.

What harvest is promised?

Lord, I want to be so saturated with your words that when I pray the words will reappear in the midst of my asking, intermingling your will with mine, and so glorify the Father. In Jesus' name. Amen.

At Home in My Love

"I've loved you the way my Father has loved me. Make yourselves at home in my love. If you keep my commands, you'll remain intimately at home in my love. That's what I've done — kept my Father's commands and made myself at home in his love."

JOHN 15:9-10

Christ sticks with us through thick and thin. There is an element of perseverance to what he does, and there is also an element of serenity. Because Christ has done it, we can do it. He provides example, motive, and energy for us to live in his ways.

How many times is "at home" used?

You, O God, are steady and firm, but I am easily shaken and recurrently restless. Establish me in your love, fix in me your purposes, so that I may without wavering live to your praise and glory. Amen.

My Joy . . . Your Joy

"I've told you these things for a purpose: that my joy might be your joy, and your joy wholly mature."

JOHN 15:11

"Come, we that love the Lord, and let your joys be known; join in a song with sweet accord, and thus surround the throne. Let those refuse to sing who never knew our God; but children of the heavenly King should speak their joys abroad."[45]

What makes you joyful?

You, O God, have introduced a new kind of joy into my life — a delight in knowing that the king of creation is making something eternal in me. "A song to our strong God! a shout to the God of Jacob!" (Psalm 81:1). Amen.

Your Life on the Line

"This is my command: Love one another the way I loved you. This is the very best way to love. Put your life on the line for your friends. You are my friends when you do the things I command you."

JOHN 15:12-13

If we get our ideas of love from journalists and entertainers, we will become hopelessly muddled. If we get them from Jesus Christ, we will have a clear and convincing pattern to follow as we obey his command to love one another.

How did Jesus demonstrate his love?

I don't know what more I need, Lord: You have both told me what you want me to do and showed me how to do it. In love you have given your life for me; now I give myself to you. Amen.

Friends

"I'm no longer calling you servants because servants don't understand what their master is thinking and planning. No, I've named you friends because I've let you in on everything I've heard from the Father."

JOHN 15:14-15

God does not turn us into robot servants so that we can help do the chores and run the errands of salvation; we become intimate friends and share the secrets of redemption.

How do friends differ from servants?

Thank you, Lord Jesus, for lifting me to where you are, for telling me your whole mind, for sharing yourself completely with me, for trusting me with your ministry, and for giving me your love. Amen.

I Chose You

"You didn't choose me, remember; I chose you, and put you in the world to bear fruit, fruit that won't spoil. As fruit bearers, whatever you ask the Father in relation to me, he gives you. But remember the root command: Love one another."

JOHN 15:16-17

Before we ever thought of God, he thought of us. Before we decided we needed God, he decided he wanted us. He has far better plans for us than any we can think up for ourselves.

Why did God choose you?

Dear God, I know you didn't choose me without having, also, some purpose for me. Show me what you have in mind—the tasks, the blessings, the acts of love that you have for me, in Jesus' name. Amen.

The World Is Going to Hate You

"If you find the godless world is hating you, remember it got its start hating me. If you lived on the world's terms, the world would love you as one of its own. But since I picked you to live on God's terms and no longer on the world's terms, the world is going to hate you. When that happens, remember this: Servants don't get better treatment than their masters. If they beat on me, they will certainly beat on you. If they did what I told them, they will do what you tell them. They are going to do all these things to you because of the way they treated me, because they don't know the One who sent me."

JOHN 15:18-21

Jesus teaches us to expect neither popularity nor applause when we serve him. Christians get support not from the world but from knowing that we are chosen by Christ for difficult service.

How do you experience the world's rejection?

God, you know how much I want everybody to like me. Especially when I do what is good, I want them to cheer me on. But that's childish; they didn't applaud Jesus, why should they do it for me as I follow him? What I need is not the world's approval, but your blessing. Amen.

Hated

"If I hadn't come and told them all this in plain language, it wouldn't be so bad. As it is, they have no excuse. Hate me, hate my Father—it's all the same. If I hadn't done what I have done among them, works no one has *ever* done, they wouldn't be to blame. But they saw the God-signs and hated anyway, both me and my Father. Interesting—they have verified the truth of their own Scriptures where it is written, 'They hated me for no good reason.'"

JOHN 15:22-25

Why do some, when confronted with the best, choose the worst? Why do people reject God in Christ? For the person who wants to do things his or her own way, who wants to live in unrestricted selfishness and unlimited pride, Jesus is bad news.

What Scripture does Jesus quote?

Lord, what you put up with from me! You patiently wait through my rebellion, my hate, my rejection—until all the energies of my sin are spent, and then receive me in love, graciously and lovingly. Thank you. Amen.

Confirm Everything

"When the Friend I plan to send you from the Father comes — the Spirit of Truth issuing from the Father — he will confirm everything about me. You, too, from your side must give your confirming evidence, since you are in this with me from the start."

JOHN 15:26-27

One way to respond to Christ is to hate him, rejecting him because he exposes our sin. Another way is to be a witness, talking to others about him in appreciation because he redeems us from our sin.

What witness do you make?

Gracious God, thank you for using me just as I am, for not waiting until I'm an expert Christian before you let me witness to your presence and lordship in my life. Keep me in readiness for the word and act that will direct another to you, through Jesus. Amen.

Rough Times Ahead

"I've told you these things to prepare you for rough times ahead. They are going to throw you out of the meeting places. There will even come a time when anyone who kills you will think he's doing God a favor. They will do these things because they never really understand the Father. I've told you these things so that when the time comes and they start in on you, you'll be well-warned and ready for them."

JOHN 16:1-4

Words can deceive or reveal. Words either unsettle us or assure us. The words of Jesus reveal and assure. They purge us of the greasy sediments of men's words and keep us from being poisoned by the lies of the world.

What words of Jesus do you remember best?

I'm not a steady person, God. I waver and slip. Use the words of your Son to rivet my will to you in loyal obedience that I may never fall away. I pray in Jesus' name. Amen.

Let Me Say It Again

"But now I am on my way to the One who sent me. Not one of you has asked, 'Where are you going?' Instead, the longer I've talked, the sadder you've become. So let me say it again, this truth: It's better for you that I leave. If I don't leave, the Friend won't come. But if I go, I'll send him to you."

JOHN 16:5-7

By repeating his message, Jesus is trying to shift their focus from the way things appear to the way they are, in Christ. It is a transition from our partial understanding to the Spirit's complete revelation.

What advantage does Jesus promise?

Lord, I get so caught up in my own plans—my childish fancies and private disappointments—that I fail to see the grand design you are working out. And then, by your grace, I see it again—a design that makes my life far richer than what I planned, more joyful than what I anticipated. Hallelujah! Amen.

Expose the Error

"When he comes, he'll expose the error of the godless world's view of sin, righteousness, and judgment: He'll show them that their refusal to believe in me is their basic sin; that righteousness comes from above, where I am with the Father, out of their sight and control; that judgment takes place as the ruler of this godless world is brought to trial and convicted."

JOHN 16:8-11

When Jesus left his disciples, he filled the gap of his absence with a new and better presence. The Holy Spirit (the "Friend," verse 7) was given to bring God's will to personal attention in regard to sin, righteousness, and judgment, three fundamental but easily overlooked realities in our lives.

What else does the Holy Spirit do?

Holy Spirit, I open myself to your presence so you can do your work: Show me my sin, create in me your righteousness, prepare me for judgment, through Jesus Christ. Amen.

Spirit of the Truth

"I still have many things to tell you, but you can't handle them now. But when the Friend comes, the Spirit of the Truth, he will take you by the hand and guide you into all the truth there is."

JOHN 16:12-13

Another work of the Holy Spirit (in addition to "Friend") is truth-telling. The father of lies has formidable opposition as the Holy Spirit keeps the word of God alive in the consciousness of each new generation.

What truth has the Holy Spirit brought home to you?

Grant, O Holy Spirit, that I may be quick to know the difference between truth and error, and then recognizing the truth, speedy to act upon it for Jesus' sake. Amen.

Deliver It to You

"He won't draw attention to himself, but will make sense out of what is about to happen and, indeed, out of all that I have done and said. He will honor me; he will take from me and deliver it to you. Everything the Father has is also mine. That is why I've said, 'He takes from me and delivers to you.'"

JOHN 16:14-15

The work of the Spirit is always practical: That which is in the Father and is revealed by the Son is applied by the Spirit. As the Spirit delivers to us the revelation of the Father through the Son, we are confronted and brought to faith.

What does the Spirit deliver to you today?

Without your Spirit, Lord, I would procrastinate endlessly. By your Spirit I am brought to daily decisions to live by your truth and to grow in your grace. Help me to respond truly, in faith. Amen.

Sadness into Gladness

"In a day or so you're not going to see me, but then in another day or so you will see me." That stirred up a hornet's nest of questions among the disciples: "What's he talking about: 'In a day or so you're not going to see me, but then in another day or so you will see me'? And, 'Because I'm on my way to the Father'? What is this 'day or so'? We don't know what he's talking about." Jesus knew they were dying to ask him what he meant, so he said, "Are you trying to figure out among yourselves what I meant when I said, 'In a day or so you're not going to see me, but then in another day or so you will see me'? Then fix this firmly in your minds: You're going to be in deep mourning while the godless world throws a party. You'll be sad, very sad, but your sadness will develop into gladness."

JOHN 16:16-20

The disciples had faced difficult times ahead. They were going to feel abandoned and desperate, betrayed and helpless. But their feelings, while authentic enough, would not be the reality. The reality was with God. They would learn not to interpret God's word by their feelings but let their feelings be interpreted (and changed) by God's word.

What did Jesus mean by "in another day or so"?

Make the word of my Lord far more real to me, O Holy Spirit, than my feelings about those words. My feelings are fickle, up one day and down the next—God's word is certain, steady, and true. Amen.

Pain

"When a woman gives birth, she has a hard time, there's no getting around it. But when the baby is born, there is joy in the birth. This new life in the world wipes out memory of pain. The sadness you have right now is similar to that pain, but the coming joy is also similar."

JOHN 16:21-22

No mature woman avoids childbirth because it is painful: The joy is worth the pain. Neither do mature Christians shun discipleship because it is arduous: All the pains have a purpose and the outcome is eternally joyous.

What pains of faith are you temporarily feeling?

God, I don't want to go through my life always looking for easy, painless paths. I want to find the true way and the straight path. I know you will give me strength to accept whatever difficulties I meet and bring me to a full life of joyous fellowship with you. Amen.

Full of Joy

"When I see you again, you'll be full of joy, and it will be a joy no one can rob from you. You'll no longer be so full of questions. This is what I want you to do: Ask the Father for whatever is in keeping with the things I've revealed to you. Ask in my name, according to my will, and he'll most certainly give it to you. Your joy will be a river overflowing its banks!"

JOHN 16:23-24

Jesus directs our faith through suffering, persecution, and pain to the completion of joy. He wants us to set our goals on the highest kind of joy and shape our prayers around that. The resurrection shows us how joy is fulfilled.

What joy has God given you?

When I encounter difficulties, Lord, help me not to be blocked by them but rather to see through them to the joy that is prepared for me. Seeking your Easter strength, help me to find your resurrection grace adequate to my need. Amen.

The Father

"I've used figures of speech in telling you these things. Soon I'll drop the figures and tell you about the Father in plain language."

JOHN 16:25

In Jesus' day most people believed there was a God, but few thought of him kindly. For those who grudgingly respected him as a far-off lawgiver or timorously feared him as an angry judge, Jesus proclaimed him as Father and demonstrated a personal relationship with him in love.

How does the word "father" change your ideas of God?

"Our Father in heaven, reveal who you are. Set the world right; do what's best—as above, so below. Keep us alive with three square meals. Keep us forgiven with you and forgiving others. Keep us safe from ourselves and the Devil. You're in charge! You can do anything you want! You're ablaze in beauty! Yes. Yes. Yes" (Matthew 6:9-13). Amen.

Directly

"Then you can make your requests directly to him in relation to this life I've revealed to you. I won't continue making requests of the Father on your behalf. I won't need to. Because you've gone out on a limb, committed yourselves to love and trust in me, believing I came directly from the Father, the Father loves you directly. First, I left the Father and arrived in the world; now I leave the world and travel to the Father."

JOHN 16:26-28

Asking "directly" defines our expectations in terms of God's love as revealed in Jesus. It is not a way of getting everything we want—a kind of license for indulging in fantasy and greed—but a means of receiving what God wills for us.

What will you ask from God now?

Father in heaven: I want many things, but need very few. Jesus said that "one thing only is essential" (Luke 10:42). Show me that one thing so that I may ask and receive, lacking nothing of what you will for me in Jesus. Amen.

Take Heart!

His disciples said, "Finally! You're giving it to us straight, in plain talk—no more figures of speech. Now we know that you know everything—it all comes together in you. You won't have to put up with our questions anymore. We're convinced you came from God." Jesus answered them, "Do you finally believe? In fact, you're about to make a run for it—saving your own skins and abandoning me. But I'm not abandoned. The Father is with me. I've told you all this so that trusting me, you will be unshakable and assured, deeply at peace. In this godless world you will continue to experience difficulties. But take heart! I've conquered the world."

JOHN 16:29-33

Jesus saw through the sudden enthusiasm of the disciples. He knew that they would falter and defect in the hours just ahead. But he didn't bawl them out; he anticipated their despair and promised his help to bring a cheerful victory in their lives.

What is the basis for the cheerful future?

You know, God, how quickly I can move from bold enthusiasm to cowering despair. Bring me through my episodes of unfaithfulness so that I may be counted among those who overcome through Jesus Christ my Lord. Amen.

Glorify Your Son

Jesus said these things. Then, raising his eyes in prayer, he said: "Father, it's time. Display the bright splendor of your Son so the Son in turn may show your bright splendor. You put him in charge of everything human so he might give real and eternal life to all in his charge. And this is the real and eternal life: That they know you, the one and only true God, and Jesus Christ, whom you sent. I glorified you on earth by completing down to the last detail what you assigned me to do. And now, Father, glorify me with your very own splendor, the very splendor I had in your presence before there was a world."

JOHN 17:1-5

Jesus concluded his conversation with his disciples and began to talk to God; he prayed. This prayer (all of chapter 17) shows what Jesus cares about most: He traces his relationship with the Father and his intentions for people.

What is Jesus' relationship with God?

Father, thank you for letting me overhear this prayer of Jesus. It shows me what prayer can be when it matures. As I pray, bring to birth in my heart the things that really count in your eyes. In Jesus' name. Amen.

The Men and Women You Gave Me

"I spelled out your character in detail to the men and women you gave me. They were yours in the first place; then you gave them to me, and they have now done what you said. They know now, beyond the shadow of a doubt, that everything you gave me is firsthand from you, for the message you gave me, I gave them; and they took it, and were convinced that I came from you."

JOHN 17:6-8

Jesus' prayer demonstrates what Friedrich von Hügel called the "deep, great fact of intercessory Prayer: that souls—all human souls—are deeply interconnected." Eternal relationships are nurtured in the exchanges between Father, Son, and the men and women "you gave me."

Who prays for you?

Lord Jesus, keep me faithful in my prayers for those you have given to me: for family and friends, for neighbors and colleagues. Let my work in prayer sustain them in their work of love. Amen.

I Pray for Them

"I pray for them. I'm not praying for the God-rejecting world but for those you gave me, for they are yours by right. Everything mine is yours, and yours mine, and my life is on display in them. For I'm no longer going to be visible in the world; they'll continue in the world while I return to you. Holy Father, guard them as they pursue this life that you conferred as a gift through me, so they can be one heart and mind as we are one heart and mind."

JOHN 17:9-11

Jesus' ministry with us is not finished when he speaks God's word and demonstrates God's presence. He continues to guide and shape our lives by his prayers of intercession on our behalf.

How do Jesus' prayers affect you?

What a difference it makes as I pray, Father, to know that Jesus is praying for me and that my prayers to you are surrounded by his prayers for me. That makes me want to pray more than ever in the name of Jesus. Amen.

Truth-Consecrated

"As long as I was with them, I guarded them in the pursuit of the life you gave through me; I even posted a night watch. And not one of them got away, except for the rebel bent on destruction (the exception that proved the rule of Scripture). Now I'm returning to you. I'm saying these things in the world's hearing so my people can experience my joy completed in them. I gave them your word; the godless world hated them because of it, because they didn't join the world's ways, just as I didn't join the world's ways. I'm not asking that you take them out of the world but that you guard them from the Evil One. They are no more defined by the world than I am defined by the world. Make them holy—consecrated—with the truth; your word is consecrating truth. In the same way that you gave me a mission in the world, I give them a mission in the world. I'm consecrating myself for their sakes so they'll be truth-consecrated in their mission."

JOHN 17:12-19

Jesus' concern for us, expressed in his prayer to the Father, is that we be set apart ("consecrated") to be examples of God's truth in the world: each Christian an instance of something that God is doing in redeeming love.

What are you set apart for?

Dear Jesus, I see what you want me to become, but I have no power in myself to produce it. I depend wholly on you to bring about the consecration you desire. Continue your prayers for me, O Christ. Amen.

One Heart and Mind

"I'm praying not only for them but also for those who will believe in me because of them and their witness about me. The goal is for all of them to become one heart and mind—just as you, Father, are in me and I in you, so they might be one heart and mind with us. Then the world might believe that you, in fact, sent me. The same glory you gave me, I gave them, so they'll be as unified and together as we are—I in them and you in me. Then they'll be mature in this oneness, and give the godless world evidence that you've sent me and loved them in the same way you've loved me."

JOHN 17:20-23

Jesus expands his concern: Not only does he care about us as individuals, he wants us to be pleasing to God as a church so that the fellowship between the Son and the Father may be reflected in harmonious intimacy among Christians in the church.

What separates you from other Christians?

Lord, when I hear you praying as ardently for my unity with the other people you love as you do for my unity with you, I am jarred loose from my private piety. Fulfill your prayers for my oneness with others. Amen.

Long Before There Was a World

"Father, I want those you gave me to be with me, right where I am, so they can see my glory, the splendor you gave me, having loved me long before there ever was a world. Righteous Father, the world has never known you, but I have known you, and these disciples know that you sent me on this mission."

JOHN 17:24-25

The ministry of Jesus is not a hastily thought-up rescue operation, instigated by God when he saw everything was going to pieces. Jesus is the consummation of an original plan for our salvation, which was set in motion "long before there ever was a world."

Compare this with Colossians 1:15-20.

My part, O God, is not to second-guess you or offer spur-of-the-moment advice to you on how to run your world. My part is to listen and accept your love, and walk in the glorious way that you have so elaborately planned for me in Jesus. Amen.

I Am in Them

"I have made your very being known to them—who you are and what you do—and continue to make it known, so that your love for me might be in them exactly as I am in them."

JOHN 17:26

A brilliant conclusion to a passionate prayer: Jesus' will for us is that we be filled with the love of God, even as he himself experienced that love. Jesus, living in us, will provide both the content and the motive for the experience.

What happens as Christ lives in you?

Lord Jesus Christ, you are the great intercessor through whom all the riches of God become available to me. Live ardently in me. Thank you for your generous love and interceding grace. Amen.

Over the Brook Kidron

Jesus, having prayed this prayer, left with his disciples and crossed over the brook Kidron at a place where there was a garden. He and his disciples entered it. Judas, his betrayer, knew the place because Jesus and his disciples went there often. So Judas led the way to the garden, and the Roman soldiers and police sent by the high priests and Pharisees followed. They arrived there with lanterns and torches and swords. Jesus, knowing by now everything that was coming down on him, went out and met them. He said, "Who are you after?" They answered, "Jesus the Nazarene." He said, "That's me." The soldiers recoiled, totally taken aback. Judas, his betrayer, stood out like a sore thumb. Jesus asked again, "Who are you after?" They answered, "Jesus the Nazarene." "I told you," said Jesus, "that's me. I'm the one. So if it's me you're after, let these others go."

JOHN 18:1-8

The garden, long a place of quiet prayer for Jesus, now is a place of strenuous temptation. Will he accept the Father's will? Will he submit to violence by those he came to save? He will and he does. Adam's disobedience (also in a garden!) is reversed in Jesus' act of obedience, and old sin becomes new righteousness.

Where is the Kidron?

I will never know, Lord Jesus, the powerful inner struggles that you endured that night; I do know that faithful prayer and a long obedience were the foundations for your victory. Use my place "over the brook Kidron" to prepare me for the testing and fit me for the final obedience. Amen.

Openly

Then the Roman soldiers under their commander, joined by the Jewish police, seized Jesus and tied him up. They took him first to Annas, father-in-law of Caiaphas. Caiaphas was the Chief Priest that year. It was Caiaphas who had advised the Jews that it was to their advantage that one man die for the people. Simon Peter and another disciple followed Jesus. That other disciple was known to the Chief Priest, and so he went in with Jesus to the Chief Priest's courtyard. Peter had to stay outside. Then the other disciple went out, spoke to the doorkeeper, and got Peter in. The young woman who was the doorkeeper said to Peter, "Aren't you one of this man's disciples?" He said, "No, I'm not." The servants and police had made a fire because of the cold and were huddled there warming themselves. Peter stood with them, trying to get warm. Annas interrogated Jesus regarding his disciples and his teaching. Jesus answered, "I've spoken openly in public. I've taught regularly in meeting places and the Temple, where the Jews all come together. Everything has been out in the open. I've said nothing in secret. So why are you treating me like a conspirator? Question those who have been listening to me. They know well what I have said. My teachings have all been aboveboard." When he said this, one of the policemen standing there slapped Jesus across the face, saying, "How dare you speak to the Chief Priest like that!" Jesus replied, "If I've said something wrong, prove it. But if I've spoken the plain truth, why this slapping around?" Then Annas sent him, still tied up, to the Chief Priest Caiaphas.

JOHN 18:12-24

It is characteristic for God to act openly and publicly. Righteousness is out in the open. Goodness takes place in a light-filled creation. It is evil that is furtively plotted behind closed doors and whispered in shadows. One strong shaft of sunlight exposes its tawdry unreality.

What was the purpose of Annas's questions?

God, help me to see and respond to what is obvious: the glories of your creation and the clarities of your revelation. I will avoid all evasive mystification and walk in the open, with Jesus. Amen.

Barabbas

Meanwhile, Simon Peter was back at the fire, still trying to get warm. The others there said to him, "Aren't you one of his disciples?" He denied it, "Not me." One of the Chief Priest's servants, a relative of the man whose ear Peter had cut off, said, "Didn't I see you in the garden with him?" Again, Peter denied it. Just then a rooster crowed. They led Jesus then from Caiaphas to the Roman governor's palace. It was early morning. They themselves didn't enter the palace because they didn't want to be disqualified from eating the Passover. So Pilate came out to them and spoke. "What charge do you bring against this man?" They said, "If he hadn't been doing something evil, do you think we'd be here bothering you?" Pilate said, "You take him. Judge him by *your* law." The Jews said, "We're not allowed to kill anyone." (This would confirm Jesus' word indicating the way he would die.) Pilate went back into the palace and called for Jesus. He said, "Are you the 'King of the Jews'?" Jesus answered, "Are you saying this on your own, or did others tell you this about me?" Pilate said, "Do I look like a Jew? Your people and your high priests turned you over to me. What did you do?" "My kingdom," said Jesus, "doesn't consist of what you see around you. If it did, my followers would fight so that I wouldn't be handed over to the Jews. But I'm not that kind of king, not the world's kind of king." Then Pilate said, "So, are you a king or not?" Jesus answered, "You tell me. Because I am King, I was born and entered the world so that I could witness to the truth. Everyone who cares for truth, who has any feeling for the truth, recognizes my voice." Pilate said, "What is truth?" Then he went back out to the Jews and told them, "I find nothing wrong in this man. It's your custom that I pardon one prisoner at Passover. Do you want me to pardon the 'King of the Jews'?"

They shouted back, "Not this one, but Barabbas!" Barabbas was a Jewish freedom fighter.

JOHN 18:25-40

The substitution of Jesus for Barabbas seems like a monstrous tragedy—a preference for mediocre evil over blazing goodness. But the substitution was not fatal, for God made an act of atonement out of it whereby Barabbas also might be saved.

How do you think Barabbas felt?

Lord, I pretend indignation at the crowd's choice of Barabbas, but I do it too, choosing dull mediocrities over blazing virtues, the familiar and comfortable ways of the world over the challenging, spirit-stretching way of Christ. Forgive me and train me in better choices. Amen.

Here He Is: The Man

So Pilate took Jesus and had him whipped. The soldiers, having braided a crown from thorns, set it on his head, threw a purple robe over him, and approached him with, "Hail, King of the Jews!" Then they greeted him with slaps in the face. Pilate went back out again and said to them, "I present him to you, but I want you to know that I do not find him guilty of any crime." Just then Jesus came out wearing the thorn crown and purple robe. Pilate announced, "Here he is: the Man." When the high priests and police saw him, they shouted in a frenzy, "Crucify! Crucify!" Pilate told them, "You take him. You crucify him. I find nothing wrong with him." The Jews answered, "We have a law, and by that law he must die because he claimed to be the Son of God."

JOHN 19:1-7

Jesus—scourged, mocked, and powerless—is still, even in the blurred vision of Pilate, the man. Just as the crowds inadvertently witnessed to Jesus' royalty, Pilate testified to his profound humanity—a complete expression of what it means to be a human being.

How are Jesus and Adam alike?

By your grace, O God, I will grow up into complete adulthood—into the measure and stature of Christ. Just as I learn the divine will from you, so I will also learn essential humanity from you, in Jesus. Amen.

Here Is Your Mother

At this, Pilate tried his best to pardon him, but the Jews shouted him down: "If you pardon this man, you're no friend of Caesar's. Anyone setting himself up as 'king' defies Caesar." When Pilate heard those words, he led Jesus outside. He sat down at the judgment seat in the area designated Stone Court (in Hebrew, *Gabbatha*). It was the preparation day for Passover. The hour was noon. Pilate said to the Jews, "Here is your king." They shouted back, "Kill him! Kill him! Crucify him!" Pilate said, "I am to crucify your king?" The high priests answered, "We have no king except Caesar." Pilate caved in to their demand. He turned him over to be crucified. They took Jesus away. Carrying his cross, Jesus went out to the place called Skull Hill (the name in Hebrew is *Golgotha*), where they crucified him, and with him two others, one on each side, Jesus in the middle. Pilate wrote a sign and had it placed on the cross. It read: "JESUS THE NAZARENE THE KING OF THE JEWS." Many of the Jews read the sign because the place where Jesus was crucified was right next to the city. It was written in Hebrew, Latin, and Greek. The Jewish high priests objected. "Don't write," they said to Pilate, "'The King of the Jews.' Make it, 'This man said, "I am the King of the Jews."'" Pilate said, "What I've written, I've written." When they crucified him, the Roman soldiers took his clothes and divided them up four ways, to each soldier a fourth. But his robe was seamless, a single piece of weaving, so they said to each other, "Let's not tear it up. Let's throw dice to see who gets it." This confirmed the Scripture that said, "They divided up my clothes among them and threw dice for my coat." (The soldiers validated the Scriptures!) While the soldiers were looking after themselves, Jesus' mother, his aunt, Mary the wife of Clopas, and Mary Magdalene stood at the foot of the cross. Jesus saw his mother and the disciple he loved standing near her. He said to his mother,

"Woman, here is your son." Then to the disciple, "Here is your mother." From that moment the disciple accepted her as his own mother.

JOHN 19:12-27

Even while doing the cosmic work of atonement, Jesus attended to domestic details: He gave his mother another son, and his disciple a new mother. The gospel creates new family ties, both of affection and responsibility, for us.

Who was the "disciple he [Jesus] loved"?

Lord, whom do you want me to love? For whom do you want me to care? Enlarge my sense of family beyond the walls of this house; increase my capacity for affectionate responsibility beyond this immediate family. Amen.

Complete

Jesus, seeing that everything had been completed so that the Scripture record might also be complete, then said, "I'm thirsty." A jug of sour wine was standing by. Someone put a sponge soaked with the wine on a javelin and lifted it to his mouth. After he took the wine, Jesus said, "It's done . . . complete." Bowing his head, he offered up his spirit. Then the Jews, since it was the day of Sabbath preparation, and so the bodies wouldn't stay on the crosses over the Sabbath (it was a high holy day that year), petitioned Pilate that their legs be broken to speed death, and the bodies taken down. So the soldiers came and broke the legs of the first man crucified with Jesus, and then the other. When they got to Jesus, they saw that he was already dead, so they didn't break his legs. One of the soldiers stabbed him in the side with his spear. Blood and water gushed out. The eyewitness to these things has presented an accurate report. He saw it himself and is telling the truth so that you, also, will believe. These things that happened confirmed the Scripture, "Not a bone in his body was broken," and the other Scripture that reads, "They will stare at the one they pierced." After all this, Joseph of Arimathea (he was a disciple of Jesus, but secretly, because he was intimidated by the Jews) petitioned Pilate to take the body of Jesus. Pilate gave permission. So Joseph came and took the body. Nicodemus, who had first come to Jesus at night, came now in broad daylight carrying a mixture of myrrh and aloes, about seventy-five pounds. They took Jesus' body and, following the Jewish burial custom, wrapped it in linen with the spices. There was a garden near the place he was crucified, and in the garden a new tomb in which no one had yet been placed. So, because it was

Sabbath preparation for the Jews and the tomb was convenient, they placed Jesus in it.

JOHN 19:28-42

"Complete" has a double meaning. It means ended—the hours of agony on the cross are over and death at hand. And it means finished—the work of redemption is wholly accomplished and eternal life begun.

What Scripture is quoted?

God, what you accomplished perfectly and completely in Jesus on the cross, accomplish in me. Complete and perfect that which you have begun, for Jesus' sake and by his grace. Amen.

I Saw the Master!

Early in the morning on the first day of the week, while it was still dark, Mary Magdalene came to the tomb and saw that the stone was moved away from the entrance. She ran at once to Simon Peter and the other disciple, the one Jesus loved, breathlessly panting, "They took the Master from the tomb. We don't know where they've put him." Peter and the other disciple left immediately for the tomb. They ran, neck and neck. The other disciple got to the tomb first, outrunning Peter. Stooping to look in, he saw the pieces of linen cloth lying there, but he didn't go in. Simon Peter arrived after him, entered the tomb, observed the linen cloths lying there, and the kerchief used to cover his head not lying with the linen cloths but separate, neatly folded by itself. Then the other disciple, the one who had gotten there first, went into the tomb, took one look at the evidence, and believed. No one yet knew from the Scripture that he had to rise from the dead. The disciples then went back home. But Mary stood outside the tomb weeping. As she wept, she knelt to look into the tomb and saw two angels sitting there, dressed in white, one at the head, the other at the foot of where Jesus' body had been laid. They said to her, "Woman, why do you weep?" "They took my Master," she said, "and I don't know where they put him." After she said this, she turned away and saw Jesus standing there. But she didn't recognize him. Jesus spoke to her, "Woman, why do you weep? Who are you looking for?" She, thinking that he was the gardener, said, "Mister, if you took him, tell me where you put him so I can care for him." Jesus said, "Mary." Turning to face him, she said in Hebrew, "*Rabboni!*" meaning "Teacher!" Jesus said, "Don't cling to me, for I have not yet ascended to the Father. Go to my brothers and tell them, 'I ascend to my Father and your Father, my God and your

God.'" Mary Magdalene went, telling the news to the disciples: "I saw the Master!" And she told them everything he said to her.

John 20:1-18

Mary was emptied of expectation, and she was devoid of hope. Every tie to Jesus was broken and every link to Jesus severed. Out of such emptiness and loss comes the fulfillment of God's promises. Friedrich Nietzsche said, "Only where graves are is resurrection."

What sorrow separates you from God?

Lord Jesus Christ, I think because you are not where I expect you that you are not anywhere; I think that because you do not appear in the way I last saw you that you are not to be seen. Yet you, praise God, are always surprising me with a resurrection appearance. Amen.

Peace to You

Later on that day, the disciples had gathered together, but, fearful of the Jews, had locked all the doors in the house. Jesus entered, stood among them, and said, "Peace to you." Then he showed them his hands and side. The disciples, seeing the Master with their own eyes, were exuberant.

JOHN 20:19-20

They supposed that the same forces that had crucified Jesus would now be directed to their destruction, and they were locked up by fear. But they were not left to such an imprisonment — Jesus released them from it with his word of peace.

Compare this with Jesus' promise in 14:27.

Too much of my life, Lord, is lived under the fearful aspect of what others think and do; stand with me and dissolve my fears, freeing me to live in your peace. Amen.

Receive the Holy Spirit

Jesus repeated his greeting: "Peace to you. Just as the Father sent me, I send you." Then he took a deep breath and breathed into them. "Receive the Holy Spirit," he said. "If you forgive someone's sins, they're gone for good. If you don't forgive sins, what are you going to do with them?"

JOHN 20:21-23

The Holy Spirit is God active in us. He is not a feeling and not a sensation, but God at work in and through us. All who believe and live in the resurrection of Jesus Christ become actual participants in the risen life.

Compare this with Jesus' promise in 14:25-31.

"Breathe on me, Breath of God, until my heart is pure, until with Thee I will one will, to do and to endure. Breathe on me, Breath of God, till I am wholly Thine, until this earthly part of me glows with Thy fire divine."[46] Amen.

Don't Be Unbelieving

But Thomas, sometimes called the Twin, one of the Twelve, was not with them when Jesus came. The other disciples told him, "We saw the Master." But he said, "Unless I see the nail holes in his hands, put my finger in the nail holes, and stick my hand in his side, I won't believe it." Eight days later, his disciples were again in the room. This time Thomas was with them. Jesus came through the locked doors, stood among them, and said, "Peace to you." Then he focused his attention on Thomas. "Take your finger and examine my hands. Take your hand and stick it in my side. Don't be unbelieving. Believe." Thomas said, "My Master! My God!" Jesus said, "So, you believe because you've seen with your own eyes. Even better blessings are in store for those who believe without seeing."

JOHN 20:24-29

Thomas was treated with great gentleness by Jesus, but yet with real firmness. His doubts were met and dealt with, but they were not made into virtues. Immaturity, while in one degree or another inevitable, is not admirable.

How are you like Thomas?

God, lead me into an Abrahamic faith that believes before it sees. Accompany me as I travel an uncertain path in the light of your certain promises and in the strong name of Jesus. Amen.

It's the Master!

After this, Jesus appeared again to the disciples, this time at the Tiberias Sea (the Sea of Galilee). This is how he did it: Simon Peter, Thomas (nicknamed "Twin"), Nathanael from Cana in Galilee, the brothers Zebedee, and two other disciples were together. Simon Peter announced, "I'm going fishing." The rest of them replied, "We're going with you." They went out and got in the boat. They caught nothing that night. When the sun came up, Jesus was standing on the beach, but they didn't recognize him. Jesus spoke to them: "Good morning! Did you catch anything for breakfast?" They answered, "No." He said, "Throw the net off the right side of the boat and see what happens." They did what he said. All of a sudden there were so many fish in it, they weren't strong enough to pull it in. Then the disciple Jesus loved said to Peter, "It's the Master!" When Simon Peter realized that it was the Master, he threw on some clothes, for he was stripped for work, and dove into the sea.

JOHN 21:1-8

The sunrise appearance of Jesus breaks in upon our lives with explosive force. Work that was futile apart from Christ becomes successful in his presence.

How did Peter know it was Jesus?

Your resurrection life, Lord Jesus, is like a sunrise in work that has lost meaning and in routines that have become pointless. Whatever my work today, I will do it in the recognition of your presence and under your command. Amen.

Net Full of Fish

The other disciples came in by boat for they weren't far from land, a hundred yards or so, pulling along the net full of fish. When they got out of the boat, they saw a fire laid, with fish and bread cooking on it. Jesus said, "Bring some of the fish you've just caught." Simon Peter joined them and pulled the net to shore—153 big fish! And even with all those fish, the net didn't rip. Jesus said, "Breakfast is ready." Not one of the disciples dared ask, "Who are you?" They knew it was the Master. Jesus then took the bread and gave it to them. He did the same with the fish. This was now the third time Jesus had shown himself alive to the disciples since being raised from the dead.

JOHN 21:9-14

The catch of fish demonstrated that the risen Christ was among them in their daily work, giving completion and meaning to it. The resurrection transforms Monday work as much as Sunday worship.

What resurrection appearances preceded this one?

Lord, in my unbelief I don't expect you to take an interest in my workday routines; your appearance is a welcome surprise, commanding, transforming, sustaining. All praise to you, risen Christ. Amen.

Yes, Master

After breakfast, Jesus said to Simon Peter, "Simon, son of John, do you love me more than these?" "Yes, Master, you know I love you." Jesus said, "Feed my lambs." He then asked a second time, "Simon, son of John, do you love me?" "Yes, Master, you know I love you." Jesus said, "Shepherd my sheep." Then he said it a third time: "Simon, son of John, do you love me?" Peter was upset that he asked for the third time, "Do you love me?" so he answered, "Master, you know everything there is to know. You've got to know that I love you."

JOHN 21:15-17

The patient persistence of Jesus' questions probed beneath the sin and guilt of Peter's recent denials (see John 18:15-27) and built a new identity as Christ's disciple. The triple affirmation of love matched and overcame the triple denial. Peter was restored.

Why was Peter singled out?

How grateful I am, Father, that you do not "treat us as our sins deserve, nor pay us back in full for our wrongs" (Psalm 103:10) but treat us with mercy and grace. Restore me to your fellowship and make me strong in your service. Amen.

What's That to You?

Turning his head, Peter noticed the disciple Jesus loved following right behind. When Peter noticed him, he asked Jesus, "Master, what's going to happen to *him*?" Jesus said, "If I want him to live until I come again, what's that to you? You—follow me." That is how the rumor got out among the brothers that this disciple wouldn't die. But that is not what Jesus said. He simply said, "If I want him to live until I come again, what's that to you?"

JOHN 21:20-23

It is not given to us to know what God is doing with others; we need to pay attention to what he is doing with us. Disciples are not permitted to gossip, even if the gossip is about God. It is enough to know that he says to us, "Follow me" (verse 19).

What did Jesus mean?

Dear God, deliver me from the curiosity that asks questions about what is none of my business. Bring me back to the point of faith where I respond to you, the place of obedience where I believe in you, and the path of love where I follow you, in Jesus' name. Amen.

So Many Other Things

This is the same disciple who was eyewitness to all these things and wrote them down. And we all know that his eyewitness account is reliable and accurate. There are so many other things Jesus did. If they were all written down, each of them, one by one, I can't imagine a world big enough to hold such a library of books.

JOHN 21:24-25

With wonderful skill and impeccable veracity, John has written what we need to know of Jesus and our salvation. He has not indulged our curiosity. He has not overloaded us with information and incident. From now on all our energy goes into belief and obedience and praise.

Do you ever find yourself wondering about the things you don't know instead of obeying the things right before you?

Lord Jesus Christ, thank you for giving me enough but not too much. Now keep me believing and obedient before this spare and inviting story. Help me to assimilate your life into my life and daily live praising your glory. Amen.

Notes

1. Charlotte Elliot, "Just as I Am," 1936.
2. Paraphrasing W. H. Auden.
3. Phillips Brooks, "O Little Town of Bethlehem," *The Hymnbook* (Presbyterian Church in the U.S., United Presbyterian Church of North America, and Reformed Church in America: 1955), 157.
4. Karl Barth, *Epistle to the Romans* (London: Oxford University Press, 1933), 380.
5. W. H. Auden, "In Memory of W. B. Yeats," *Collected Poems*, Edward Mendelson, ed. (New York: Random House, 1976), 198.
6. F. W. Faber, "O Come and Mourn with Me a While," *The Hymnbook*, 174.
7. Sören Kierkegaard, *Purity of Heart Is to Will One Thing* (New York: HarperOne, 1956), 53.
8. Isaac Watts, "So Let Our Lips and Lives Express," *The Hymnbook*, 250.
9. Samuel Johnson, "Father, in Thy Mysterious Presence Kneeling," *The Hymnbook*, 326.
10. T. S. Eliot, "Choruses from 'The Rock,'" *The Waste Land and Other Poems* (London: Faber & Faber, 1972).
11. James Montgomery, "Prayer Is the Soul's Sincere Desire," *The Hymnbook*, 331.
12. Katharina von Schlegel, "Be Still My Soul," *The Hymnbook*, 318.
13. Shakespeare, *Hamlet*, act 5, scene 2, line 147.
14. Watts.
15. Edward Mote, "My Hope Is Built on Nothing Less," *The Hymnbook*, 313.
16. Anonymous.
17. Jane Laurie Borthwick, "Come, Labor On," *The Hymnbook*, 248.
18. William C. Dix, "Come unto Me, Ye Weary," *The Hymnbook*, 233.
19. *The Book of Common Prayer*, Protestant Episcopal Church, 1928.
20. Cecil Frances Alexander, "Jesus Calls Us," *The Hymnbook*, 234.
21. Henry van Dyke, "Joyful, Joyful, We Adore Thee," *The Hymnbook*, 31.
22. Theodulph of Orleans, "All Glory, Laud, and Honor," *The Hymnbook*, 171.
23. R. Robinson, "Come, Thou Fount of Every Blessing," *The Hymnbook*, 322.
24. *Pilgrim Hymnal* (Boston: Pilgrim Press, 1958).
25. Sarah E. Taylor, "O God of Light, Your Word, a Lamp Unfailing," *The Hymnbook*, 217.
26. John Ellerton, "This Is the Day of Light," *The Hymnbook*, 70.
27. G. Bernanos, *Diary of a Country Priest* (Garden City, NY: Image Books, 1954), 164.
28. James Montgomery, "According to Thy Gracious Word," *The Hymnbook*, 373.
29. G. Croly, "Spirit of God, Descend Upon My Heart," *The Hymnbook*, 207.
30. Charles Wesley, "Love Divine, All Loves Excelling," *The Hymnbook*, 337.

31. Anonymous.

32. H. Bonar, "Blessing and Honor and Glory and Power," *The Hymnbook*, 125.

33. Mary A. Lathbury, "Break Thou the Bread of Life," *The Hymnbook*, 219.

34. Ancient Greek hymn "O Gladsome Night."

35. George Matheson, "Make Me a Captive, Lord," *The Hymnbook*, 264.

36. Calvin, *Institutes of the Christian Religion*, vol. 1 (Philadelphia: Westminster John Knox Press, 1960), 72.

37. Taylor.

38. Henry W. Baker, "The King of Love My Shepherd Is," *The Hymnbook*, 100.

39. "All Saints," *The Book of Common Prayer*, Protestant Episcopal Church, 1928.

40. Walter Chalmers Smith, "Immortal, Invisible, God Only Wise," *The Hymnbook*, 82.

41. John Donne, *Devotions upon Emergent Occasions* (Ann Arbor: University of Michigan Press, 1959), 141.

42. Faber, 174.

43. This is title of a booklet by Robert Boyd Munger, originally published in 1954.

44. Charles Wesley, "Thou Hidden Source of Calm Repose," *The Hymnbook*, 356.

45. Isaac Watts, "Come, We That Love the Lord," *The Hymnbook*, 344.

46. Edwin Hatch, "Breathe on Me, Breath of God," *The Hymnbook*, 206.

About the Author

EUGENE H. PETERSON is a pastor, scholar, author, and poet. He has written more than thirty books, including Gold Medallion Book Award winner *The Message: The Bible in Contemporary Language*. He earned his BA in philosophy from Seattle Pacific University, his STB from New York Theological Seminary, and his MA in Semitic languages from Johns Hopkins University. In 1962, Peterson was a founding pastor of Christ Our King Presbyterian Church in Bel Air, Maryland, where he served for many years before retiring in 1991. He is Professor Emeritus of spiritual theology at Regent College in Vancouver, British Columbia, and lives in Montana with his wife, Jan.

More devotional readers!

Holiness Day by Day
Jerry Bridges

Looking for a deeper devotional? *Holiness Day by Day* offers teaching from Jerry Bridges' best writings on spiritual transformation. Each entry is quick and easy to read, stimulating personal growth.

978-1-60006-396-1

The J. I. Packer Classic Collection
J. I. Packer

Contained in this yearlong daily reader are the writings and teachings of J. I. Packer. You will read excerpts from his best and experience the warmth of feeling and appreciation that will only be reinforced and enhanced by his timeless words of daily wisdom and encouragement.

978-1-61521-574-4

How Great Is Our God

How Great Is Our God is a beautiful collection of 312 inspiring readings with devotions that explore the nature of our loving God. Reading it is like taking a master class with some of the greatest Christian thinkers of the last century: Andrew Murray (*Waiting On God and Working for God*), A. W. Tozer (*The Pursuit of God*), Jerry Bridges (*Trusting God*), and many more.

978-1-61521-730-4